# Child protection
The therapeutic option

**Acknowledgements**

We wish to thank all those who shared their knowledge and expertise with us in the BAAF/BASPCAN working party meetings. They were doctors, lawyers and social workers from statutory authorities, voluntary agencies and private practice and included representatives from Childline, the Crown Prosecution Service, the Family Rights Group, the National Children's Bureau, the National Foster Care Association, the NSPCC and the Metropolitan Police.

We have appreciated the support of the honorary officers of BASPCAN in preparing this book and would also like to thank the Baring Foundation for their generous grant which funded the meetings of the Working Party and contributed towards the production costs of this book.

**A note about the editors**

Deborah Cullen is a solicitor and has worked for BAAF as Co-ordinator of the BAAF Legal Group since 1983. She also has experience of criminal and matrimonial legal work.

Daphne Batty is a social worker and had worked for BAAF as Co-ordinator of the BAAF Medical Group from 1985 until 1995, when she retired. She was previously responsible for adoption and fostering services in two London boroughs.

# Child protection
## The therapeutic option

Edited by
Daphne Batty and
Deborah Cullen

**B** *r i t i s h*

**A** *g e n c i e s*

*f o r* **A** *d o p t i o n*

*a n d* **F** *o s t e r i n g*

Published by
**British Agencies for Adoption & Fostering**
(BAAF)
Skyline House
200 Union Street
London SE1 0LX

© BAAF 1996

Charity registration 275689

British Library Cataloguing in Publication
Data
A catalogue record for this book is available
from the British Library

ISBN 1 873868 28 6

Designed by Andrew Haig & Associates
Typeset by Gilbert Composing Services
Printed by Progressive Printing UK Ltd

# Contents

# Foreword

*Marion Miles*

*Dr Marion Miles, Chair of the BAAF Medical Group, is Consultant Community Paediatrician at the Medical Centre, Parkside Health Trust. She is medical adviser to two inner London boroughs and also to a voluntary adoption agency.*

In any one child protection case a large number of people can become involved: children, parents, foster carers, social workers, doctors, psychiatrists, therapists, teachers, police, lawyers and judges. Each of these has a different role to play and they may conflict, thus exposing the child to even greater distress than that already experienced. Any move to change child protection procedures must, therefore, be a consolidated move. Everyone concerned must be involved in and committed to the changes made.

At a BAAF Medical Group seminar in 1992, considerable concern was expressed regarding the emphasis put on investigation in child protection at the cost of providing effective support to the abused children and their families. Against this backdrop of growing dissatisfaction, it seemed appropriate to bring into play BAAF's traditional practice of drawing together the various professions involved in child care in order to explore a way forward. In 1993, BAAF joined forces with BASPCAN (British Association for the Study and Prevention of Child Abuse and Neglect) and held two workshops with participants from different disciplines and various organisations, all concerned with child protection. Our aim was to examine in greater detail the current procedure-driven process and to consider possible alternatives.

This book voices the deliberations of those participants. It also reflects a subsequent widening of the debate, culminating in the publication by the Department of Health of *Child Protection: Messages from research*[1] which echoes many of the themes considered here. The points of view of all the relevant professions are represented, together with those of the children and families. There is a remarkable degree of unity in the desire for change, but, as Ruth Gardner observes in her final chapter, there are no simple answers to the complex questions posed. Our intention in this book is to inform the continuing debate.

In Chapter 1, Christine Hallett examines the history and function of child protection services in Britain. Following the publication of various inquiry reports, the focus has been on identifying the abuse and giving consideration to prosecution rather than on identifying the support needed by the family. She argues for the reverse of this trend if we are to promote the welfare of the child and family needs.

David Spicer takes a critical look at the impact of the legal system. He highlights both the misuse of resources and the damage done by the expectation that there is necessarily evidence to prove serious allegations. Both he and Joan Robinson, in the following chapter, point to the need to acknowledge that prevention of all abuse is impossible. Given the problems identified it is not surprising, therefore, that the current demand for a lighter touch in child protection will be difficult to achieve and will require a real commitment to the welfare of children rather than the demands of current procedures.

Joan Robinson identifies key points at which a shift of emphasis away from the investigative model can have a significant effect. She advocates giving greater responsibility for problem solving to the family, with better family support strategies to achieve this, and suggests ways of helping social workers to become supporters rather than investigators.

Jane Tunstill and Celia Atherton consider the terms "family support" and "partnership" indicating that the recent research now offers less threatening ways of providing support and child protection. In their consideration of partnership they give useful examples of planning systems which allow debate between users and providers, bearing in mind that participation has to be facilitated for this process to be successful.

Margaret Lynch examines the role of paediatricians and other health professionals. She stresses the importance of identification of health needs and considers the difficulties which may be encountered because of recent health service organisational changes. She recognises and deplores reluctance on the part of some paediatricians to become involved in child protection and highlights the dangers of an unbalanced medical input which, as in other disciplines, concentrates on investigation and confirmation of abuse rather than the provision of continuing support. Paediatricians have an important role in explaining the health contribution to families and colleagues and ensuring that children and families are kept well informed. The delivery of health care needs to be flexible to encourage compliance and should be clearly defined in the child protection plan.

Judith Trowell considers the conflicts that exist between children's rights and their needs. Adults must accept the responsibility for ensuring that needs are met and must also accept that this will not necessarily comply with the child's own immediate wishes. Frequently there is confusion in trying to balance needs with rights. It follows that professionals require considerable skills and should work within a supportive framework if abuse within the system is to be avoided. Given that many children want to stay in an abusive home once the abuse stops, the logic of providing whole family therapeutic support is unavoidable.

Gerrilyn Smith discusses how children should be protected and who is responsible for providing protection. She advocates the development of a wider protection network involving non-abusing parents and the community while acknowledging that perpetrators will attempt to infiltrate this network or circle. We are reminded that recovery involves the inner, closest circle of protectors and requires their belief that abuse has taken place if progress is to be made.

Ena Fry highlights the contribution of foster carers as members of a professional team. The range and advantages of foster care are discussed together with the difficulties carers face in dealing with sometimes openly rejecting children. She describes the support and training that carers need – from assessment through to placement and onwards – in order to ensure safe caring. She also pays particular attention to the situation of foster families who are subjected to allegations of abuse. The work of the National Foster Care Association (NFCA) mediation service is discussed and good practice guidelines are outlined.

Rachael Hetherington looks to European models, offering a new slant on resolving our problems in child protection. She describes a research project, using paired English and French social workers, in which it becomes apparent that the French system has greater flexibility, with a sharper focus on the family's needs. The differences which facilitate a more therapeutic approach include greater resources, the different use of the judicial system, with much less emphasis on investigation, and a belief in the ability of families to change for the better.

Sarah Borthwick and Barbara Hutchinson describe the Confidential Doctor system in Belgium where the police are not routinely involved in child abuse cases. This approach encourages families to seek help voluntarily; with the removal of the risk of prosecution, denial is reduced and therapy facilitated. The process generates an air of optimism and families rarely separate. Realistically there is acknowledgement of the universal capacity for abuse but also an expectation of improvement for most families. However, the authors retain some reservations about the system and these are explored.

In essence, this book is about policies, procedures and strategies for change. Whatever our professed concern, it is easy enough in discussing strategy to lose sight of the child at the centre of the procedural labyrinth. But those of us involved in child protection are sadly familiar with individual children who have been subjected to repeated interviews and examinations prior to court hearings, their parents disempowered and antagonised, their home lives disrupted, and longer and longer delays before the provision of any support that can be described as therapeutic. We are witnesses to the consequent damage. Contributors to this anthology, writing from different perspectives, believe that resources can be redirected and attitudes changed in order to offer a better deal to abused children and those closest to them. The chapters demonstrate how this can be done. The cost to the children, and by implication to their children, is otherwise too great to contemplate.

### Reference

1  Department of Health, *Child Protection: Messages from research*, HMSO, 1995.

# 1    From investigation to help

*Christine Hallett*

*Christine Hallett is Professor of Social Policy and Director of the Social Work Research Centre at the University of Stirling, Scotland. She has published extensively in the field of child welfare.*

**This chapter explores aspects of the functioning of child protection services. It suggests that the system is "front loaded", that is, the efforts of social workers and many others in the interprofessional network are focused extensively and intensively on the investigative stage. The early stages of case construction are currently dominated by a forensic, evidence-gathering concern with abusive incidents. The author outlines the case for some refocusing of activity on broader family needs.**

### The investigation of abuse referrals

High priority is given in British child protection services to the initial investigation of allegations of child abuse. Since the 1970s, central government guidance and local procedures devised by the then Area Review Committees have governed the processes. The investigative phase is characterised by a high degree of interagency activity as checks and inquiries are made of the local professional networks. These involve not only social workers but routinely also doctors, health visitors, teachers and police, as is discussed more fully below.

The allocation of child abuse referrals for investigation is accorded high priority within social services/social work departments, as reflected in the following observation:

> 'Ultimately, the most dangerous thing is not going out and having a look at it . . . My own view is that the responsibility for the child's safety lies with the investigating agency . . . I don't think we, as a department, can avoid that responsibility.'[1]

Much larger numbers of children are referred on grounds of abuse to social services departments than are registered. Gibbons et al's study[2] of almost 2,000 referrals in eight local authorities in England reported that significant numbers were diverted from the system at early stages after interagency checks. Only 15 per cent of the original sample proceeded to registration following an initial child protection conference. However, this study suggests that, despite pressing needs, children and parents who were weeded out at an early stage, particularly when the allegations were of neglect, were often offered no services.

Research evidence[3,4] suggests that the focus of concern in the investigative stage is to establish as clearly as possible the status of the case: Is this a case of child abuse? What has happened? In particular, who did what to whom? Is there sufficient evidence to prosecute? It appears that less attention is paid in the process of investigation to an assessment of the strengths and weaknesses of the family or to its broader needs for help and support. One respondent summarised it as follows:

'. . . what we're getting more recently and more frequently is an allegation of abuse; all the checks are done, the medical is done and a case conference is called and, if you are lucky, a social worker will visit the family and let them know that and that's it.'[5]

**The role of the police**
The forensic mode of response to allegations of abuse reflects in part the much increased role of the police in initial investigation. This represents a profound change from the position following the discovery or, more properly, the "rediscovery" of child abuse in the 1960s and 1970s when the concern was predominantly with non-accidental injuries. For example, the circular of guidance issued in 1974 following the Maria Colwell inquiry listed the professions and agencies which a case conference should normally include as follows:

a) persons having statutory responsibilities for the continuing care of the child, eg. the appropriate senior member of the social services department, the consultant in charge of the patient's medical care;

b) persons concerned with the provision of services likely to be relevant to the case, eg. area social worker, voluntary agency representatives, family doctor and health visitor, psychiatrist treating child or parents, day nursery matron;

c) persons with information regarding the child and his [or her] family, eg. family doctor and health visitor (if not included under (b)), social workers including probation officers in previous and present contact, paediatrician and members of medical and nursing staff.[6]

Health and social services staff dominate the list and the police are included in the category of 'others who may be invited as appropriate'.

In 1971, the Association of Chief Police Officers stated in their evidence to the Select Committee on Violence in the Family:

'Every case must be regarded with a degree of suspicion, and it is incumbent upon the social services, medical profession, hospitals, etc, to ensure that the police are involved in a case at the earliest possible stage. The police service must be involved in all cases of violence.'[7]

Their complaint at the time was that this was not happening.

Parton[8] has characterised the subsequent change as one from a socio-medical to a socio-legal discourse. Concerns about sexual abuse have altered the interprofessional balance of power, partly because of the ambiguities, and sometimes the absence, of medical evidence in these cases, and partly because the propensity, or at least the desire, to prosecute appears to be greater in cases of sexual than physical abuse.[9] The position is now that the police are at the core of initial investigations. A senior social services manager summarised it thus:

'I think, in many ways, our closest colleagues are the coppers. They are in it up to their necks as we are.'[10]

This is epitomised by the joint investigation, although there is evidence in practice of varying degrees of joint working.[11] What is not in dispute is that substantial amounts of police and social work time are devoted to investigations. Government guidance outlines the purpose of police involvement as follows:

'Police involvement in cases of child abuse stems from their primary responsibilities to protect the community and bring offenders to justice. Their overriding consideration is the welfare of the child. In the spirit of *Working Together*, the police focus will be to determine whether a criminal offence has been committed, to identify the person

3

or persons responsible, and to secure the best possible evidence in order that appropriate consideration can be given as to whether criminal proceedings should be instituted.'

The government guidance goes on to outline the factors to be taken into account in deciding whether to prosecute:
'The decision whether or not criminal proceedings should be initiated will be based on three main factors: whether or not there is sufficient substantial evidence to prosecute, whether it is in the public interest that proceedings should be instigated against a particular offender, and whether or not it is in the interests of the child victim that proceedings should be instituted.'[12]

The ordering of these three factors is interesting, given the primacy accorded to the welfare of the child in the earlier paragraph. A child-welfare orientation is more marked in the central government guidance issued to the police in 1988, in a Home Office Circular entitled *The Investigation of Child Sexual Abuse*. It concluded:
'It is essential that all professional agencies concerned with the protection and welfare of children work together in harmony and towards a common goal . . . the success of the police intervention . . . is not to be measured in terms of the prosecutions which are brought, but of the protection which their actions bring to children at risk.'[13]

Although it appears that national data about the outcomes of police involvement are not available, research studies suggest that the rate of prosecutions is low. Table 1[14] shows the position in one police authority in England.

Moran-Ellis et al in a study of investigations of sexual abuse cases conducted in 1989 and 1990 reported prosecution rates of 12 per cent in one research site and seven per cent in another.[15] Creighton's study reported that between 1988 and 1990 criminal prosecutions occurred in 17 per cent of a sample of 1,732 registered child sexual abuse cases and in nine per cent of a sample of 2,786 physical cases.[16] The contribution of law enforcement to the protection of children is therefore limited. Whether the routine and extensive involvement of the limited resource of social work time is best

4

*Table 1*

**Outcome of police investigations of referrals of child abuse in one police authority**

|  | 1989 | | 1990 | |
|---|---|---|---|---|
|  | No. of referrals | | No. of referrals | |
| No further action | 2214 | (72%) | 2469 | (62%) |
| Caution | 181 | (6%) | 223 | (6%) |
| Prosecution | 436 | (14%) | 251 | (6%) |
| Outstanding at the year end | 234 | (8%) | 1008 | (26%) |
|  | 3065 | (100%) | 3951 | (100%) |

spent on investigative activity is clearly a matter for debate.

The dominant focus on forensic concerns in initial investigations continues in initial child protection conferences for cases which proceed to that stage. In these, it appears that much attention is paid to the precipitating "incident" or immediate cause for concern and to the outcome of initial medical examinations and police or social work inquiries.[17, 18, 19, 20] The criteria for placing a child's name on the child protection register in England and Wales are that there is, or there is likelihood of, significant harm *and* an interagency child protection plan is required. However, as one respondent observed:

'I think they take decisions about registration and then formulate the child protection plan, where, in reality, it ought to be the other way round.'[21]

There is some evidence that the formulation of the child protection plan is accorded relatively little priority in initial conferences. Farmer and Owen,[22] for example, found that in a sample of 120 observed conferences, an average of only nine minutes was devoted to discussion of child protection plans in conferences which lasted on average over an hour. A similar picture emerges from scrutiny of conference minutes in my own research. One respondent observed:

'I've had the sense at several case conferences that you've spent two hours working out, well discussing whether or not registration should take place, discussing the police investigation, where it might go from here or whatever; people are exhausted by the time you get to that stage and often I think there isn't a proper child protection plan worked out.'[23]

The emphasis in initial child protection conferences upon investigation and the labelling and classification of "the abusive incident" is a feature, and possibly a requirement, of a system with clear categories of registration, the potential involvement of the criminal justice system in respect of abusers, and the need for evidence in respect of compulsory measures of care. It is reported to be a much less marked feature in systems such as those in Holland, parts of Germany and parts of Belgium where the approach is more voluntaristic and therapeutic, and where there is little criminalisation of child abuse. Christopherson,[24] for example, reports that in the Dutch case notes he studied, details of the abuse were sketchy because the abusive incident was of secondary importance to the family's overall functioning and needs. Lampo and Marneffe[25] describe how, by comparison with the British system, little attention is paid in a treatment centre in Brussels to the abuse itself. Instead, the focus is on the child's needs and the family's functioning.

These are difficult and contentious matters. Earlier generations of social workers were criticised for their alleged naïvety and propensity to believe implausible accounts of injuries sustained by children, and for failing to probe in sufficient depth and detail what had actually occurred, for example, in the case of Maria Colwell.[26] Social workers were also castigated for paying insufficient attention to child *protection*, most trenchantly in the Jasmine Beckford report.[27] It is unlikely that children's welfare will be promoted if they are not protected from harm. Investigation of what has occurred to assess the degree of risk seems to be a prerequisite for this.[28] Purvis, for example, stresses the need to explore the situational nature of the abusive act or acts in great detail, covering their history and circumstances and the motivations and opportunities of the alleged abuser in order to assess future risk. However, it is unlikely that the welfare of children will be promoted without simultaneous consideration of the broader needs for help and support for them and their families. There is a balance to be achieved. While no doubt practice varies, recent research evidence as reviewed above suggests that there is a need to sharpen the focus on assessing child and family welfare, alongside child protection. This could be accomplished without significant additional resources.

### The content of child protection plans

A refocus would need to be reflected in the content of child protection plans. Even before the implementation in 1991 of the Children Act 1989, with its preference for voluntary rather than compulsory measures of care, most children on child protection registers and subject to a child protection plan lived at home under voluntary supervision. This was the case for 74 per cent of the children in Creighton's study[29] and for 96 per cent in the research studies reviewed on behalf of the Department of Health.[30]

The contents of the plans and their capacity to contribute to the safety and well-being of children is therefore crucial. There have been relatively few studies of the efficacy of such plans, not least because of the difficulty of evaluating outcomes and of tracing linkages between cause and effect in this as in other human service endeavours.[31] In a typical year in England some 30,000 children's names are removed from child protection registers as no longer in need of an interagency protection plan.[32] This rate of turnover suggests that, at least when viewed from a professional perspective, there is some success.

However, while this is some evidence of a degree of success in the goal of child *protection* there is less optimism about the capacity of intervention to provide effective help to children and parents, many of whom have a wide range of needs. There may be several reasons for this, including the lack of needs assessment outlined above. It appears that following registration, the responsibility for continued intervention rests principally and sometime exclusively with social workers. In one third of the cases in Farmer and Owen's sample,[33] the only intervention recommended was social work contact. In a study of primary school aged children on the child protection register, there was little specification in child protection plans of ongoing involvement by paediatricians, psychologists, psychiatrists, other specialist treatment resources, schools or general practitioners. Gough et al's study[34] of 202 children on the child protection register in a Scottish region noted the low level of interagency work and recorded surprise at finding 'such low levels of formal involvement of other agencies in what is meant to be an interdisciplinary monitoring system'. Creighton and Noyes[35] noted the central role of social workers and the possible over-reliance of other professions upon their role.

There is, in general, a sharp reduction in the investment of interagency time and resources at the stage of working with children and parents to help solve their problems once the crisis, and possibly the excitement, of investigation and initial conference has passed. This is in marked contrast to the relatively successful engagement of the interagency network in referral and initial investigation. Yet the intervention phase is precisely the point where interagency effort needs to be concentrated, since investigation and registration in themselves are likely to do little to enhance children's well-being or the capacity of their parents to care for them. It appears that greater efforts need to be made to engage a wider range of professions and services in providing ongoing help. Elsewhere in this collection, for example, Margaret Lynch outlines the important role of continued paediatric involvement.

## Implementation of child protection plans

If a real impact is to be made on family functioning and children's well-being following their involvement with child protection procedures, it is likely that greater attention will need to be paid not just to the formulation and content of interagency plans but also to their effective implementation. Given the importance accorded to initial investigation and the relentless need to prioritise work, it is, perhaps, unsurprising that plans are not always implemented. As one social services manager observed:

> 'We're not bad at the investigation, we're not bad at coming up with a plan to protect the child. What we are bad at is following it up.'[36]

There is no avoiding the issue of the shortage of resources in considering follow-up, whether of facilities such as day care, family centres, specialist fostering, specialist treatment services or the basic resource of time for social workers and the professionals involved. Respondents within and outwith social services spoke with a weary acceptance of the severe resource shortages in my recent research, as the following quotations indicate:

'I think we've come to the point now where we recognise that yes, we don't have the resources, and I guess we don't fight about those anymore. I think there's a general understanding that everybody's in the same boat and we wish to be able to undertake therapy in a totally different way if only we had the resources. And that phrase is said many times, "if only we had the resources we could do this, that and get it right," but we don't.

'There comes a point where you've got to call a moratorium on blame and you've got to say in order to provide a service of child protection in this area, this area needs that amount of resources. Blow your rate support grant, whether it's a Labour controlled council or Liberal or Conservative, it doesn't matter. If you've got children who are hurt then this is what needs to be provided. As a department, the range of resources available to support families and treat abuse in families is pitiful.'[37]

Other difficulties can include a lack of family commitment to the plans and the bewildering pace of change and complexity in the lives of many of the families involved which calls for flexibility in implementation and for reassessment. However, research, notably that by Thoburn et al,[38] suggests unsurprisingly that family commitment can be increased by successful policies and practices or the involvement of children and parents in decision making.

## Conclusion

This chapter has suggested that, from one perspective, the systems established in the UK for the referral and initial investigation of cases of child abuse appear to work reasonably well, particularly for serious cases. This is a relatively clear and routinised division of labour with extensive engagement of the interagency network. However, the focus is principally upon the investigation of a specific incident or presenting condition with a view to allocating responsibility, determining case status (in particular the need for registration) and to an assessment of risk. While these are required, it appears that the system may be poorly targetted and that a broader assessment of the needs of the children and their families are necessary if effective help and support are to be provided to enhance children's welfare as well as to protect them from significant harm.

## References

1 Hallett C, *Interagency Co-ordination in Child Protection*, HMSO, 1995.

2 Gibbons J, Conroy S, and Bell C, *Operating the Child Protection System* HMSO, 1995.

3 See 1 above.

4 Farmer E, and Owen M, *Child Protection Practice: Private risks and public remedies*, HMSO, 1995.

5 See 1 above.

6 Department of Health and Social Security, *Non-accidental Injury to Children*, Lass L, 74:13, 1974.

7 House of Commons 329-11, *First Report from the Select Committee on Violence in the Family*, Session 1976-77, Vol II Evidence, 1977.

8 Parton N, *Governing the Family: Child care, child protection and the state*, Macmillan, 1991.

9 Creighton S, *Child Abuse Trends in England and Wales 1988-90*, NSPCC, 1992.

10 See 1 above.

11 Moran-Ellis J, Conroy S, Fielding N, and Tunstill J, *Investigation of Child Sexual Abuse: An executive summary*, University of Surrey, 1991.

12 Home Office, Department of Health, Department of Education and Science, Welsh Office, *Working Together under the Children Act: A guide to arrangements for interagency co-operation for the protection of children from abuse*, HMSO, 1991.

13 Home Office, *The Investigation of Child Sexual Abuse*, Circular 52/1988, 1988.

14   See 1 above.

15   See 11 above.

16   See 9 above.

17   cf, for example, Hilgendorf L, *Social Workers and Solicitors in Child Care Cases*, HMSO, 1981.

18   Department of Health, Social Services, *Inspection of Child Protection Services in Rochdale*, Manchester: DHSS1 NW Region, 1991.

19   See 4 above.

20   See 1 above.

21   See 1 above.

22   See 4 above.

23   See 1 above.

24   Christopherson J, 'European child abuse management systems', in Stevenson O (ed), *Child Abuse: Public policy and professional practice,* Harvester Wheatsheaf, 1989.

25   Lampo A, and Marneffe C, *Prevention of Child Abuse and Neglect: Child protection or mere registration,* unpublished paper, 4th European Conference on Child Abuse and Neglect, Padua, 1993, Italy.

26   Department of Health and Social Security, *Report of the Committee of Inquiry into the Care and Supervision provided in relation to Maria Colwell,* HMSO, 1974.

27   London Borough of Brent, *A Child in Trust: The Report of the Panel of Inquiry into the circumstances surrounding the death of Jasmine Beckford,* London Borough of Brent, 1985.

28   Purvis H, 'Dangerous Clients: Further observations on the limitation of mayhem', *British Journal of Social Work*, 18:6, 592-609, 1988.

29   See 9 above.

30 Department of Health, *Child Protection: Messages from research*, HMSO, 1995.

31 Cheetham J, Fuller R, McIvor G, and Petch A, *Evaluating Social Work Effectiveness*, Open University Press, 1992.

32 Department of Health, *Children and Young People on Child Protection England Registers year ending 31 March 1992*, Government Statistics Service, 1993.

33 See 1 above.

34 Gough D, Boddy M, Dunning N, and Stone F, *A Longitudinal Study of Child Abuse in Glasgow, Volume 1: the children who were registered*, University of Glasgow: Social Paediatric & Obstetric Research Unit, 1987.

35 Creighton S, and Noyes P, *Child Abuse Trends in England & Wales 1983-87*, NSPCC, 1989.

36 See 1 above.

37 See 1 above.

38 Thoburn J, Lewis A, and Shemmings D, *Paternalism or Partnership? Family involvement in the child protection process*, HMSO, 1995.

# 2 An injudicious approach to child protection

*David L Spicer*

*David L Spicer is a barrister and the Chair of the British Association for the Study and Prevention of Child Abuse and Neglect (BASPCAN).*

**This chapter considers a legal view of current approaches to child protection, the misuse of scarce resources, and the limitations of current practice. The author argues that a change in emphasis is required in order to serve the best interests of the child.**

### The need for change: is the process of law an obstacle?

Recent research findings should be considered within the current child protection environment and its development since the legislative overhaul of the child welfare framework in England and Wales in 1991. What is the context in which multi-professional work is currently being undertaken? What are the principal influences moulding the nature and direction of those services? What is the scope for a change of approach on the scale which the research suggests as desirable?

Effective and safe change is likely to occur best within an environment in which the services are operated by people who are confident in the exercise of their responsibilities, who feel they have the support of both their establishment and the community, and who are able to operate with authority, forming appropriate judgements while acknowledging risks which may be inevitable.

Staff involved in child protection work recognise the thrust of the research findings. They are already aware of the shortcomings of the current approach and will welcome the permission the research may afford them to work more effectively. However, there are powerful influences which may inhibit the adoption of a different approach.

At present, child protection practitioners across all agencies and disciplines suffer from low morale, from feelings of vulnerability and isolation, from a perceived lack of support and from the effect of increasing and persistent denial of their expertise. Commitment is high but cynicism among this group is extensive, particularly with regard to existing systems and, especially, the negative impact of legal processes. The functioning of the legal processes and the approach of the courts have encouraged the criminalisation of child protection. The concept of culpability is becoming paramount, and highly inappropriate misapplication of resources is extensive.

Among the expectations when child welfare legislation was revised were reaffirmation of the paramountcy of the welfare of the child, reduction in the former legalistic approach, clarification and simplification of the sources and provisions of child care law, encouragement of a co-operative approach, and removal of contentious over-reliance on the courts as a mechanism for resolving concerns over the future of children. After an initial period of inactivity following the implementation of the Children Act 1989, there has been a perceptible extension of judicial influence into the operation of the child welfare system. The approach of the courts and the treatment of cases have an impact well beyond the courtroom and stretch into both processes and practice. For example, current attitudes towards the interviewing of children owe little to the collective wisdom of child-centred professionals and more to the application of judge-made rules and inflexible principles of evidence. A far more legalistic approach has developed. There is an increasingly complicated system of child care law (hidden within the volumes of law reports which have mushroomed in this field) and an environment in which every aspect of decision-making has the potential for litigation. No area is immune from judicial interpretation and comment.

### How legislative intent can be thwarted

A number of recent developments illustrate how policies behind legislation have been distorted by judicial interpretation. There has been application of traditional judicial attitudes and also reaction to contemporary public concerns. The principle of the paramountcy of the welfare of the child, set out in the first sub-section of the first section of the Children Act, appears to practitioners to state clearly an essential and binding principle, that when a court determines any question with respect to the upbringing of a

child . . .
'. . . the child's welfare shall be the court's paramount consideration.'[1]

Despite its clarity, when it becomes difficult to apply, the principle appears to be subordinate to other interests. Sub-section 1 has been held not to apply to an application for authority to place a child in secure accommodation. The reasoning to support this judicial gloss on the legislation is that:
'. . . S25(4) is to be found later in the scheme of the Act.'[2]

and that the principle laid down in Section 1:
'. . . was not designed to apply to Part III of the Act.'[3]

Furthermore,
'It followed that whilst the child's welfare would be a consideration of great importance, it was not paramount for the purpose of Section 25.'[4]

The dominance of the requirement of the criminal justice system over child-centred principles similarly persists as the "interests of the child" are set against the "public interest" in ensuring a fair trial for an adult defendant. Decisions on the disclosure of sensitive material relating to a child victim's background, or the exposure of a child to the potentially damaging experience of criminal proceedings are made by avoiding acknowledgment of any "public interest" in the protection of vulnerable children. For example, a father's defence solicitor wished to interview his sons to discover from them how much, if anything, they had seen of an alleged assault by the father on their mother which was the subject of criminal proceedings against the father. This was even though 'the boys would clearly want to be spared the ordeal of such an interview'.
'That had to be weighed against the advantage of a fair trial for the father.'[5]

In a similar case the court, considering an application in family proceedings, concluded that:
'It did not follow that this was a matter relating to the children's upbringing to which S1(1) of the Act would apply. The interests of

15

justice in permitting the father's defence to be properly prepared should come first.'[6]

Despite long-standing concerns over delays in finalising public law proceedings and the impact of such delay, in cases in which serious criminal proceedings are pending, there should be:
'. . . exceptional circumstances that might require a child's long-term future to be arranged in care proceedings before a criminal trial is heard.'[7]

Such examples suggest to child-centred practitioners that the paramountcy principle, originally intended to assert children's interests, is unlikely to prevail against traditionally important concepts and interests. Practitioners view this with increasing concern, particularly as in addition, their involvement in the processes often leads to a denial of their expertise and a denigration of their skills. There is also failure to understand that the games played out in the courtroom influence the future child protection system.

**The effects of denigration of expertise**
Persistent challenge and criticism of anyone's ability is often self-fulfilling. Many of those working within public authorities and carrying out direct work with vulnerable children are moving away from child protection work and into less risky services, to consultancy or to the much "safer" environment of adult services. Often they are replaced by newly qualified staff. Many are avoiding involvement in areas of work where there is a high risk of extensive legal proceedings. They see a commonsense approach abandoned in favour of the complicated application to decision-making of legal rules and insistence on the involvement, in almost every aspect of the process, of costly "experts" who have no continuing responsibility.

**A misuse of scarce resources?**
Involvement in the legal system exposes staff to the scandal of scarce resources being used to service expensive and inappropriate decision-making mechanisms. The training of lawyers, the tradition of the judiciary and the administration of the courts are designed to deal with the determination of historical events. They are ill-equipped to deal with ever

changing circumstances, the functioning of human relationships, and the fine judgements – requiring constant review – that form the basis of work with vulnerable children and families. In particular, they are ill-equipped to deal with the experience of an abused child gradually and tentatively disclosing the extent of abuse suffered.

Very occasionally the courts declare care proceedings to be "non-adversarial". This reflects a policy behind the legislation. Guidance and Regulations issued pursuant to Section 7 Local Authority Social Services Act 1970 on enactment of the Children Act 1989 set out a clear expectation:

'The Rules of the court which regulate the proceedings across all three tiers of jurisdiction have been designed to promote a non-adversarial style in court.'[8]

It was also expected that the court would play a more inquisitorial role, reflected by the power to make orders of its own motion:

'Under the Act, the courts have an independent duty to do what is best for the child. If the courts are to discharge that duty, often they will have to take an active part in the proceedings rather than simply acting as umpires between the contending parties.'[9]

Neither of these paragraphs reflects the current conduct of proceedings in public law cases. Contention over every issue is permitted as advocates respond to the clear expectation of the Court of Appeal that

'those making allegations must discharge the burden of proof,'[10]

and the House of Lords that

'. . . he who asserts must prove.'[11]

Proceedings are now far more adversarial than those conducted under the previous legislation. They also involve more people whose own interests may lie in the exaggeration of contentious issues. Naturally, this has an impact on the application of resources. This has even attracted adverse comment from time to time from the House of Lords and the Court of Appeal:

'The costs of well over £2 million incurred in this case, and the time required to hear it, were excessive. It did not reflect credit on those who managed the case and perhaps on those who presented it. It might have been better for the family and the public who funded this expense, if some of the money had been directly spent upon the family instead of the protracted court proceedings.'[12]

'The level of separate representation of parties, all at public expense, was a feature of the appeal. Separate solicitors and senior and junior counsel appeared for each of the mother, father and the mother's guardian *ad litem*. There was no significant difference between their causes.'[13]

This case involved five Queen's counsel and five junior counsel, none of whom had less than 25 years' experience.

Is it appropriate for such costs to be incurred to determine whose interests should be paramount in a case involving a teenage mother with a difficult and disruptive background and her newly born baby? This is at a time when local authority budgets for children's services are being reduced substantially. The resources available for the therapeutic requirements of a vulnerable child and family are a fraction of those required to determine who is to exercise parental responsibility in an individual case.

### 'The more improbable the event, the stronger must be the evidence'

Arguably most damage has been done to the cause of child protection by legal decisions relating to the standard of proof required for a court to make findings of fact in child abuse cases. A line of authorities in the Court of Appeal have strengthened the view that the more serious the allegations made, the more cogent must be the evidence in order to establish, as a matter of fact, that an allegation is proved. As the focus of proceedings shifts from the child's situation to the adult's conduct, the stamp of the criminal jurisdiction, culpability, and negative perceptions of child protection systems have been encouraged. The standard of proof required has been reinterpreted by the House of Lords:

'. . . the more serious the allegation, the less likely it is that the event occurred, and hence the stronger should be the evidence before a court concluded that the allegation is established on the balance of probability.

'Although the result is much the same, this does not mean that where a serious allegation is an issue the standard of proof required is higher . . . The more improbable the event, the stronger must be the evidence that it did occur before, on the balance of probabilities, its occurrence will be established.'[14]

In the same case Lord Browne-Wilkinson, a dissenting Law Lord, expressed concern that the House, in supporting this approach,

'. . . may establish the law in an unworkable form to the detriment of many children at risk.'[15]

And in another dissenting opinion Lord Lloyd of Berwick expressed the view that:

'It would be a bizarre result if the more serious the anticipated injury . . . the more difficult it became for the local authority to satisfy the initial burden of proof and thereby, ultimately, if the welfare test is satisfied, secure protection for the child.'[16]

Nevertheless, the more serious the concerns and therefore the more vulnerable the child, the more difficult it is to satisfy even the threshold test necessary before the protection of that child can be considered. These principles also ensure that child protection inquiries and assessments necessarily emphasise contentious "allegations" and encourage in perpetrators of abuse an interest in persistent denial. The most vulnerable, for example, the very young or children with learning difficulties, are therefore those most unlikely to receive protection.

Here was an opportunity for the House of Lords to adopt a strong child-centred approach consistent with the philosophy of the legislation. Why should the finding of facts in establishing a threshold, designed to give rise to a protective jurisdiction, not be determined on the basis of what is more likely than not, that is, simply on the balance of probabilities? Is it not reasonable, at least, that if concerns satisfy such a test, the burden should pass to those responsible for providing a safe and caring environment for a child to show that they can do so? The failure to prove a fact to the required standard requires an assumption to be made that it positively did not occur:

'. . . an alleged but unproved fact, serious or trivial, is not a fact for this purpose.'[17]

19

In the reality of child protection work suspicions and the accumulation of factual material which would not lend themselves to dissection and subjection to strict probative analysis, nevertheless often form the basis of very serious concerns and decisions in relation to a vulnerable child. Many workers involved in the inquiries held following child abuse tragedies have been severely criticised for failing to take account of circumstances which would not have been capable of strict factual proof according to the judicial test.

Lord Browne-Wilkinson questioned whether the principles set out by the majority of Law Lords were consistent with the intention of the legislature:

> 'After a long hearing, a judge has reached the conclusion on evidence that there is a "real possibility" that her evidence is true, i.e. that she has in fact been gravely abused. Can Parliament really have intended that neither the court nor anyone else should have jurisdiction to intervene so as to protect (the child) from any abuse which she may well have been enduring? I venture to think not.'[18]

A number of the cases recently considered by the Court of Appeal illustrate the application of the principles.

### Case

A young child had died in a family and this death was suspected to be due to non-accidental causes.

> 'The local authority had to establish the primary facts of past harm on the balance of probabilities. But the more serious the allegation, the more convincing was the evidence needed to tip the balance in respect of it.'[19]

Short of murder, the allegation was the gravest that could be made against a parent, and the local authority fell short of the required standard. The parents, in this case, declined the judge's invitation to agree to a family assistance order.

### Case

A five-year-old girl was underweight, emaciated, severely dehydrated and had suffered multiple bruising on the body, renal failure and duodenal haematoma. There was a failure to seek medical help. The local authority alleged the damage was caused by a punch from the mother's cohabitee.

'The local authority and those who supported them had to establish the primary facts of past harm on the balance of probabilities. But the more serious the allegation, the more convincing was the evidence needed to tip the balance in respect of it.'[20]

The more serious allegations were not proved to the standard required.

The facts behind the recent House of Lords case quoted above,[11] highlight the difficulties of this approach for local authorities, other agencies and children, and the impact which then extends through the child protection system.

## Case

A 15-year-old girl alleged sexual abuse by her stepfather over eight years, involving rape, buggery and oral sex and was rejected by her family. Her accounts to social workers, police, other professionals and carers were consistent. She gave evidence in criminal proceedings which relied on her testimony. The jury reached a not guilty verdict after a few minutes' consideration. Lack of corroboration was a feature of the case. Unusually, the girl also gave evidence in the civil proceedings, seeking to protect the younger children remaining in the household.

The alleged abuser was found by the judge in the civil proceedings to be unreliable. The mother had been imprisoned for falsely alleging indecent assault by a social worker and was found by the judge to have known or suspected that something had been going on and to have chosen the alleged perpetrator in preference to her daughter. She was found by the judge to have lied in at least three relevant respects in the witness box.

The following extracts from the judgement give a flavour of the judicial approach at first instance.

'The social services have made up their minds that she is speaking the truth, but then they always believe the complainant . . .'

As to the alleged abuser and the mother:
'I have seldom been less impressed by a witness. If the second respondent (stepfather) had to prove that there was not sexual abuse, the matter would be no contest, but the question is, disbelieving as I do both the mother and the second respondent on a number of important matters, can I reach the conclusion which is appropriate to the local authority's plan for the child. After all, it does not follow that because the two respondents are telling material lies I can be satisfied nevertheless that CH (the complainant) is telling the truth.

'Is it sufficient for me to find that there is a real risk that she is telling the truth and may well have been abused or must I go further and be satisfied on the appropriate standard of proof that she has in fact been so abused?

'I must find a higher than ordinary standard of proof although how much higher that standard must be, may in any given case be problematical. Here the charges are clearly of the most serious nature. I cannot be sure to the requisite high standard of proof that CH's (the complainant's) allegations are true. That is far from saying that I am satisfied the child's complaints are untrue. I do not brush them aside as the jury seems to have done.

'If it were relevant I would be prepared to hold that there is a real possibility that her statements and her evidence are true.'

The judge directed himself that as the required standard of proof was not satisfied, he was required to find that the abuse had not occurred. The Court of Appeal dealing with the matter held the following:
'All the judge can do is assess the risks of what may happen . . . there must be an evidential basis for that. Fanciful risks will not do.
'The standard of proof is the balance of probabilities but the more

serious the allegations the more cogent the evidence necessary to tip the balance.'[21]

The Court of Appeal found that the judge had 'applied the correct test'. The House of Lords, by a majority of three to two, supported this approach.

Leave to appeal to the House of Lords had initially been refused, but was subsequently granted on petition to the House itself. The local authority then had a difficult decision to make. Mounting such appeals is costly and, in the current climate, comparisons have to be realistically made between the potential cost of mounting an appeal against the continued employment of, perhaps, three social workers for a year. In this event, an appeal was pursued because of the continuing identified risk to the siblings, and the importance of the principles under consideration.

The approach inherent within the system is apparent. There is no allowance for, or accommodation of, the special nature of child protection cases, nor for the secretive nature of abusive behaviour and vulnerability of the child. The seriousness of the impact on the alleged perpetrator determines the approach rather than the seriousness of the risk to the child. Lord Browne-Wilkinson, dissenting in the House of Lords, did grasp the issue:

'Child abuse, particularly sex abuse, is notoriously difficult to prove in a court of law. The relevant facts are extremely sensitive and emotive. They are often known only to the child and the alleged abuser.'[22]

**The impact of these principles**
This approach has a potentially damaging effect throughout the functioning of the child protection system. Is it realistic to expect that those with most responsibility for implementing the legislation can, with confidence, gather information, interview the people involved, and assess the facts in the light of the esoteric language of the courts? Are they entitled to conclude that abuse has occurred or is likely to occur on standards of proof less than those set down by the House of Lords, knowing that such conclusions may not be supported in the event of a challenge? What

incentive does an abuser have to acknowledge abuse when the potential to establish that abuse is so unreliable? How realistic is it to encourage children to disclose abuse in the expectation that they will be protected?

Is it appropriate to encourage children to speak fully and openly of the extent of abuse they may have suffered when the more serious the matters they allege, the less likely they are to be believed in court?

A judgement as to the establishment of significant harm or the likelihood of it is a pre-condition to a child's name being placed on the child protection register. Is it appropriate for such a finding to be made on a different standard of proof from that insisted upon by the courts? Is the court's standard appropriate in relation to protective multiagency arrangements?

Is this the appropriate standard to be applied to findings of fact and the provision of services within the legislation generally or is it a special standard applicable only to Section 31 of the Children Act? The House of Lords case[23] illustrated this problem.

Can the complainant in that case be provided with services under Part III of the Children Act as a "child in need", including therapy for sexual abuse after a court has refused to find as a matter of fact that sexual abuse has occurred? Is therapy to be provided on the basis of abuse having occurred or on the basis of fantasy or lies on the part of the child? Is it open to the local authority to require the co-operation of other agencies in the provision of services pursuant to Section 27 or may those agencies decline on the basis that there has been a failure to establish the occurrences of the sexual abuse? Is it appropriate for the younger children within the father's household to continue to be the subject of a multiagency child protection plan and for their names to remain on the register, the precondition being the likelihood of significant harm, when the courts have declined to support that likelihood?

It is not surprising that in this climate the placing of a child's name on the child protection register is increasingly seen not positively, with a high standard of appropriate services made available to the child and family, but rather negatively, reflecting a finding of culpability. It is very difficult for professionals working within the judicial context to comply with the hope expressed within the statutory guidance to the effect that the provision of child protection services should not be seen as a stigma and the recipients of the service regarded as customers. Placing a child's name on the child protection register becomes something to be avoided. The removal of a child's name from the register is held out as an incentive to encourage improvement of performance by those perceived to be "culpable". Both are inevitable in a system owing much to the field of criminal investigation and prosecution.

**The court's attitude to child protection professionals**
The concentration on the establishment of narrow allegations is bound to distort the attitude of child protection professionals who must form judgements based on a range of factors, many of which are incapable of strict legal proof. Furthermore, many staff appearing in court find that the judicial processes seldom confirm their authority to act or provide assistance in condemning poor child care practice. Judicial criticism, comment and guidance on child protection systems fill the pages of the law reports. These are meant to be acted upon by professionals, but the reports lack similar directives on appropriate child-centred standards to be expected of carers who exercise parental responsibility.

Professionals as witnesses comment upon the derogatory manner in which they have been treated while giving their evidence. This is in contrast to "experts" who may be called or, indeed, to those against whom findings of serious child abuse have been made. It is common for witnesses with day-to-day experience of child care matters to be exposed to several hours of meticulous cross-examination, undermining their evidence, their authority and often their integrity. They are questioned by people who receive more for the conduct of that case than the witness may earn in the course of a year. There appears to be little or no perception of the impact which these matters have on the conduct of the case following conclusion of the proceedings, especially on the worker's relationship with individual members of the families concerned.

Does it improve the quality of child protection services if, as in one case, a community care assistant is exposed on consecutive days to cross-examination by Queen's counsel, during the course of which differences in the compilation of her daily and weekly record were highlighted and exaggerated? After an immediate period of sick leave, this worker left her employment, rather than risk a repetition. Thus the experience of many years work with vulnerable children and families was lost.

**The misapplication of expertise**

Recently, there has been some emphasis from the courts on seeking to restrict the numbers (previously increased) of "experts" involved in child care cases. Inherent in their involvement is the denial that professionals carrying out statutory functions are capable of forming appropriate judgements in the very areas required by statute. If a particular level of expertise is required to resolve issues brought to court, should not the same level of expertise be applied to cases which, perhaps by chance alone, have not?

Interviewing and interpreting the experience of a child alleged to have been abused is recognised as a highly skilled task. Those responsible for working with these children could well be confused by the court's attitude to their skills. Where allegations of sexual abuse were made against a father:

'The guardian *ad litem* was extremely unwise to venture an opinion of the likelihood of sexual abuse having occurred.'[24]

and faced with allegations of sexual abuse a guardian *ad litem*:

'... should always seek expert advice on the interpretation of controversial material relating to allegations of sexual abuse.'[25]

However, a judge hearing the direct testimony of a child alleged to have been abused giving evidence in child care proceedings, assumes to him or herself the ability to interpret that testimony and to reach conclusions on the truth or otherwise of the child's account. Furthermore, in the criminal jurisdiction, jury members, selected from the electoral register at random, are expected to view video tape evidence and listen to the direct testimony of child witnesses and to asses the truthfulness and reliability of that testimony. That a sophisticated approach is expected of jury members is illustrated by the Court of Appeal's recent direction. This states that when juries request to view for a second time video tape evidence of a child witness, they must indicate whether this is in order to hear again what the child has said (in which case the judge might read from his/her notes of evidence) or to observe how the child has given evidence (in which case the tape could be viewed again in open court).

Experts involved in legal processes are necessarily absent from their normal professional practice. The increasing complexity, length and evidential requirements of both criminal and care proceedings not only reduce the financial resources available for application to the child care system generally, but also concentrate existing expertise on relatively few cases.

Panels of guardians *ad litem* were initially expected to feedback their improved expertise, thus leading to an improvement in standards generally. It was anticipated that guardians would either continue in practice while acting as guardians or would return to practice. The way the service has developed, however, has ensured that this interaction rarely occurs and that panels have become a further drain on the expertise of front-line practitioners.

## Conclusion

Within this environment, how can the resources so unsatisfactorily applied to servicing legal processes be redirected towards a more therapeutic approach to vulnerable children and families? The Department of Health[26] draws on recent research to argue for "a lighter touch" in child protection cases and a change of emphasis from "investigation" to "inquiry". This will only be achieved if there is acknowledgement of the impact of the legal system as it operates at present. The answer does not lie in better education of lawyers and the judiciary on the harm which can be caused to children by involvement in these processes. Perversely, better informed and better educated lawyers have led to more significant undermining of children's credibility, resulting from better informed lawyers pursuing the interests of their adult clients.

A change of emphasis is required in order to serve the best interests of the child. We must acknowledge that resources are more effective if applied to therapeutic or preventive work than if applied to the forensic resolution of disputes. We must also acknowledge that removing resources and expertise from direct work with children and families is more likely to lead to inappropriate judgements and miscarriages of justice. This is exactly what the application of principles of law are expected to prevent. Bringing about a change involves a real commitment to the welfare of children rather than to the servicing of the ever increasing demands of present procedures. Impact can be made by clear and strong statements from those well qualified within the system, showing a reluctance to co-operate in procedures clearly operating against the interests of children.

## References

1  The Children Act 1989.

2  *M* v *Birmingham City Council* (1995) 1 FCR 50.

3  See 2 above.

4  *Re M* (Secure Accommodation Order) (1995) 1 FCR 418.

5  *Re F* (1995) 2 FCR 200.

6  *Re M* (1995) 2 FCR 643.

7  *Re S* (1995) 2 FCR 697.

8  The Children Act 1989: *Guidance and Regulations*, Volume 1, para 17, HMSO, 1991.

9  *An Introduction to the Children Act 1989*, para 1.51, HMSO, 1989.

10  In *Re H and R* [1995] 1 FLR 643.

11  In *Re H and R* [1996] 1 FLR 80.

12  *Re W (M)* (1994) 1 FCR 162.

13  *Birmingham City Council* v *H* (No.3) (1994) 1 FCR 896.

14  See 11 above. Lord Nicholls of Birkenhead.

15  See 11 above. Lord Browne-Wilkinson.

16  See 11 above. Lord Lloyd of Berwick.

17  See 11 above.

18  See 11 above at p.83.

19  *Re P* (1994) 2 FLR 751

20  *Re M (A Minor)* (Care Proceedings: Appeal) (1995) 1 FCR 417.

21  See 10 above.

22   See 11 above.

23   See 11 above.

24   *B* v *B* (1994) 1 FCR 809.

25   See 24 above.

26   Department of Health, *Child Protection: Messages from research*, HMSO, 1995.

# 3 Social workers – investigators or enablers?

*Joan Robinson*

*Joan Robinson is a freelance Social Work Consultant who has worked for many years as a local authority Social Work Manager in adoption, fostering and child protection.*

**This chapter questions the appropriateness of social workers as investigators of abuse. It reports on recent research into outcomes of child protection and suggests alternative courses of action for Area Child Protection Committees and Social Services Departments.**

Social work has subscribed to a fallacy – that child abuse can be predicted, and therefore prevented. As a result, complex systems of information gathering, checks and balances and monitoring have evolved. The Department of Health has sponsored a range of research projects (listed at the end of this chapter), and some outcomes have been reported. Wendy Rose, the Assistant Chief Inspector, speaking at the Sieff Foundation Conference in September 1994,[1] signalled the Department of Health's views of the need to change the emphasis from child protection to the promotion of welfare for families in need. Two of the most significant messages emerging from research findings are that previous assault and neglect are the most reliable predictors of child abuse, and that child protection systems are not making children safer. In some instances, the systems themselves are abusive.[2]

As there is little definite evidence that abuse can be predicted, it follows that attempts to prevent abuse may be based on false assumptions. Social workers, whose intention is to prevent children being harmed, may be working from such false assumptions, which in turn lead to a perception that we are responsible for children being abused. If we accept the premise that abuse can be prevented by us, we are consequently held responsible when it occurs. Yet we are not and cannot be responsible for what parents do to their own children. We should expose this myth and be honest with ourselves, the families with whom we work, and the media, about what we can realistically do.

What often happens in practice is that one-off incidents or observations are recorded. The judgement of the social worker is crucial in then deciding what action to take. Cleaver and Freeman's research[3] suggests that social workers' decisions to take up allegations of abuses are influenced by many factors. These include such things as how long they have been a social worker; their own life experiences and training; how specific the referral was; who had made the referral, in particular, the status of the referrer; and significantly, the parents' attitude and willingness to co-operate.

The workers' judgement is also shaped by professional views and practice. These have developed not as a result of careful analysis of outcomes, but largely in response to political pressure following child deaths and subsequent abuse inquiries. Keating's research[4] shows that the majority of families on child protection registers are poor, or unemployed, or from minority ethnic backgrounds, or headed by a lone parent; sometimes a combination of these factors exists. This suggests that families who are living in poverty and deprivation are being held individually responsible for economic and social circumstances beyond their control.

Thorpe[5] suggests that social workers are making moral judgements from the premise of a class-based value system about good parenting. The registration category of neglect can be construed as a criticism of parenting rather than a description of poverty. If this is true, and poverty with all its many disadvantages is at the root, then the political dimension is also inescapable, and, as Parton says,[6] social services are faced with applying a plaster to a never-healing wound.

One way to avoid this happening is for the community to take responsibility for promoting basic living standards and child safety rather than the individual being regarded as neglecting or failing to protect the child. (Chapter 7 by Gerrilyn Smith in this collection emphasises this point, particularly in relation to sexual abuse.)

Not only can social work intervention fail to protect children from being killed, it also can actually add further distress and emotional damage.[7] Social work practice has become focused on investigating allegations, accumulating evidence and monitoring parental performance. In pursuit of protection for the child, a critical mindset towards parents can and does cause workers to remove children in the hope that alternative care will be better. It only rarely is. The benefits of removing children from an unsatisfactory home are often offset by the separation from family, friends, school and all the familiar networks and routines of a child's life.

While some children who have to be separated from their families are likely to get quality substitute care, other children in local authority care may be further abused by their carers and by the system itself. They may suffer emotional scars as a result of their separation from family and their subsequent experiences in the care system.

**The way forward**

While the issues are complex, there are key points at which a change of focus can have a significant impact.

*The social worker at the point of contact*

The focus of the social worker's assessment at the point of contact is crucial. If the emphasis is on investigating, evidence-gathering and critical analysis of parental performance, it is likely to undermine the parent. If it is directed towards finding out what can give the child a safer, happier, more fulfilled life, then it can open up a process which will enable the family to use help, and also protect the child. This means accepting that social workers cannot contain every risk, and that abuse is often unpredictable. Key questions need to be asked, such as: 'What has to happen for this child to lead a safe and fulfilling life?', and 'What do the parents need so that they can achieve this?', and 'How will they get what they need?' This approach can enable social workers to play a positive role in promoting the abilities and strengths within family networks. The shift in emphasis is from problem-analysis: abuse, risk, failure (to attend appointments and so on), to focusing on family strengths: empowerment, development of parental skills, and activating support networks. The choice of words is important: abuse covers anything from a smack to killing a child, and its use can trigger a complex set of responses and procedures.

*People in other agencies*

Social services departments have become lead agencies in child protection, and often a repository for other agencies' anxieties. It is unreal and unsafe for social workers to be regarded as the only people with responsibility to protect children. We need to open up the debate from within Social Services Departments via Area Child Protection Committees and other joint groups with people who work with families in need. Often people working in voluntary agencies, schools, and health services, for example, have known these families over many years and understand the stresses in their lives. These people are well placed to contribute to a web of support within the community. The message is that everybody involved with the family can use their own judgement and consider what they can do to contribute towards a concerted plan of support for the family.

*Who decides? Family Group Conferences*
Another key point is that at which the social worker decides what the problem is and what action to take. The responsibility for these decisions belongs most realistically with the family itself. The idea of Family Group Conferences is being tried in this country, after a marked success in New Zealand. Briefly, the model works as follows: a meeting is convened with the family network of a child believed to be in need of care or protection. The professionals, having shared their concern, withdraw from the meeting, leaving the family network with the responsibility of formulating plans for its own child. These plans then form the basis of negotiation with the professionals involved.

There is much work to be done in bringing the model into practice, but the principle it embodies is significant and could contribute towards the shift of emphasis in child protection work.[8]

*The child protection system*
Although the current debate stresses the need for a change of focus, there are some situations where child abuse *has* to be investigated. The aims of the work which follows the social worker's assessment of the family should be clearly stated. Gibbons[9] suggests this formulation:
- Only children at risk of significant harm, and none other, should enter the system and be investigated in a lawful way.
- Children on the register should have specific interagency protection plans which are regularly reviewed and are appropriate to their protection.

- Children on the register should be protected from further significant harm and the effects of previous harm on their development should be assessed.

When an investigation must go ahead and legal action is being considered, the family's *current needs* should continue to be addressed.

*Developing family support*
The high political profile of child protection has attracted resources, and any shift of focus to family support has to address this. A rescuing policy, which has removed children from families rather than keeping families together, has resulted in workers with particular skills in family assessment and training for parenting being employed in substitute family services, such as fostering and adoption teams. These workers spend much of their time assessing substitute families' strengths and weaknesses, supporting them through challenging life-events, and training them to cope with difficult behaviour, to understand child development and, in effect, to be good parents. The change of focus to family support will require some lateral thinking about the best use of existing resources. Social work resources in homefinding could perhaps be more productively aimed at supporting families in need.

In addition, if less time is spent on the investigative process and procedures, social workers will be freer to concentrate on work to support families in need.

*Department of Health*
With the backing of research, the Department of Health could speak out and dispel the myth that social workers can save children from harm. Wendy Rose[10] has made a significant contribution to the debate about the changes needed in child protection. The Department of Health sets standards for the quality of child protection work and has a central influence on the services delivered by Social Services Departments. Inquiry reports into child abuse can in themselves appear to blame social workers, and have led to more procedures. By modelling a different approach, the Department of Health could help to lift the unrealistic burden

of responsibility from the shoulders of social workers, thus giving them the confidence to take a more supportive approach to work with families without the fear of destructive criticism.

## Conclusion

There is a groundswell of opinion from research, from the political climate and from practice experience which points to the need for change in emphasis in child protection work. The people at the receiving end are alienated by an approach whose outcomes do not seem to justify the means. While there are many strands to this complex tapestry, there are significant points at which changes can be made. At a local, interagency and national level, the shift in emphasis can have an impact. The language used has a significant influence on attitudes and such phrases as 'promotion of family life', 'access to life's opportunities', and 'recognition of parental skills' can influence future action. The emphasis on defining problems is pathologising, labelling and demoralising. It is more effective to stress what we can achieve, and what the strengths are in the family.

Social workers who feel criticised and battered by angry defensive families would prefer to be genuinely involved, listening and engaging in the promotion of better lives for children and families. The practice implications raise the challenge of how to help social workers become enablers rather than investigators while keeping alive their ongoing assessment of risk. It might be helpful to:

- identify more clearly when investigation should take place;
- decide whether investigation and enabling intervention are compatible;
- decide who should carry out these tasks.

Such work is more likely to gain credibility and attract resources than the present system, provided that outcomes can be stated clearly. However, it is important not simply to equate greater family support with the prevention of abuse. By recognising that there are no certain predictors and that some children will be harmed, the systems that we put in place must aim to improve the chances of a satisfactory family life for those with whom social workers come into contact.

## References

1   Rose W, *An Overview of the Developments of Services: The relationship between protection and family support and the intentions of the Children Act 1989*, Department of Health Paper for Sieff Conference, 5 September 1994.

2   Gibbons J, Gallager B, Bell C, and Gordon D, *Development after Physical Abuse in Early Childhood: A follow-up study of children on protection registers*, HMSO, 1995.

3   Cleaver H, and Freeman P, *Parents' Perspectives in Cases of Suspected Child Abuse*, HMSO, 1994.

4   Keating T, *Child Neglect in an Inner London Borough*, Unpublished, 1994.

5   Thorpe D, *Evaluating Child Protection Programmes*, Lancaster University, 1995.

6   Parton N, *Governing the Family: Child Care, Child Protection and the State*, Macmillan, 1991.

7   See 2 above.

8   Family Rights Group, *Family Group Conferences: A report commissioned by the Department of Health*, HMSO, 1994.

9   See 2 above.

10   See 1 above.

**Child protection research sponsored by the Department of Health**
*Main studies*

Birchall E, and Hallett C, *Working together in Child Protection*, HMSO, 1995.

Cleaver H, and Freeman P, *Parents' Perspectives in Cases of Suspected Child Abuse*, HMSO, 1994.

Farmer E, and Owen M, *Child Protection Practice: Private risks and public remedies*, HMSO, 1995.

Hallet C, *Interagency Co-ordination in Child Protection*, HMSO, 1995.

La Fontaine J, *The Extent and Nature of Organised and Ritual Sexual Abuse of Children*, HMSO, 1994.

Monk E, *Descriptive and Treatment Outcome Studies of Families with a Diagnosis of Child Sexual Abuse*, HMSO, 1995.

Sharland E, Jones D, Aldgate J, Seal H, and Croucher M, *Professional Interventions in Child Sexual Abuse*, HMSO, 1995.

Smith M, and Grocke M, *Normal Family Sexuality and Sexual Knowledge in Children*, Royal College of Psychiatrists/Gorkill Press, 1995.

Smith M, Bee P, Heverin A, and Nobes G, *Parental Control within the Family: The nature and extent of parental violence to children*, paper forthcoming from Thomas Coram Research Unit.

Thoburn J, Lewis A, and Shemmings T, *Paternalism or Partnership? Family involvement in the Child Protection Process*, HMSO, 1995.


*Related studies*

Kelly L, Regan L, and Burton S, *An Exploratory Study of the Prevalence of Sexual Abuse in a Sample of 16–21 Year Olds*, University of North London (previously Polytechnic of North London), 1991.

The Research Team, Queens University, Belfast, *Child Sexual Abuse in Northern Ireland: A research study of incidence*, Greystone Press, 1990.

Waterhouse L, Pitcairn T, McGhee J, Secker J, and Sullivan C, 'Evaluating Parenting in Child Physical Abuse', in Porterhouse L, *Child Abuse and Child Abusers*, Jessica Kingsley, 1993.

# 4 Family support and partnership
## The law demands – does practice respond?

*Jane Tunstill and Celia Atherton*

*Jane Tunstill is Professor of Social Work Care Studies at Keele University. She has a background in child care social work and social work teaching. Her particular research interests are in the area of family support, and she has recently undertaken two Department of Health commissioned studies on 'Children in Need' with Jane Aldgate, and a national study for NCVCCO of the role of voluntary child car agencies.*

*Celia Atherton is Director of Family Rights Group, a national charity working to improve the law, services and attitudes towards families whose children are in need of family support, or are involved with child protection, or are looked after by the local authority.*

**The current era of child care has seen an increase in the use of the terms "family support" and "partnership", which are enshrined in the law and guidance. This chapter examines how close professionals come to making these words a true description of child care today. It emphasises the responsibility of practitioners, local authorities and central government to respond to the implications of these terms, accepting an inevitable degree of risk as well as the potential for positive outcomes.**

It is probably the case that each era of child care policy can be identified by the language in vogue at the time, although a cynic might suggest the term "jargon" as more accurate. If future historians should adopt such a literary approach, then the 1980s and 1990s will be particularly notable for the use of the terms "family support" and "partnership". Both, like many phenomena, are reactive in that they have their origins in the apparent deficiencies of earlier approaches. Both sound appealing. Both are vulnerable to the charge that they mean what people want them to mean, rather

38

than conveying an absolute and objective message. It is, therefore, necessary to start this chapter with a brief introduction to the terms before going on to examine ways in which they might interact in a positive way.

The Children Act 1989 introduced a new legislative framework for family support, based on a duty to provide services for children in need and their families (Section 17). This new duty differs in several ways from the earlier legislation (Section 1 of the Children and Young Persons Act 1963 and the Child Care Act 1980), and these differences present both advantages and challenges to implementation of the duty on the basis of partnership. There is now, undoubtedly, a broader definition of local authority powers to assist families, and these powers are dissociated from a specific concern with preventing reception into care. Both of these developments ought to offer far greater scope for imaginative policy and practice.

On the other hand, there is a new emphasis on providing services to 'children in need and their families' rather than to a potentially larger but undifferentiated population, and it seems from evidence so far available that this potential for targeting could create pitfalls. Alongside these changes, both the Children Act and the NHS and Community Care Act require the development of a common way of working with clients/users.*

The common way of working under the Act is to be based on partnership between practitioners and users, on the empirical basis that:

'A number of the elements of 'partnership practice' are directly related to effective problem solving or to effective protection: work is more effective if it is specifically addressed to problems defined jointly with the users . . . benefits to users are greater if they participate in decision making about allocation of services, and the quality of decision making is enhanced . . .'[1]

The danger is that policy makers, practitioners and the public will assume an automatic and inevitable fit between "family support" and "partnership". Ironically, this (false) assumption could hamper policy and practice

---

* There is a debate about the use of words like clients/users. For example, many young people and parents associate the term user with substance abuse and prefer other words to describe their relationship with social workers. Agencies need to listen to the views expressed by people with whom they work.

development: while there has already been a professional and legal debate about the appropriateness and feasibility of partnership in the context of protection work,[2] relatively little attention has been paid to applying the concept consistently to family support policy and practice. On the contrary, research evidence so far on the implementation of Part III of the Act suggests that the picture is far from reassuring.[3] There is no room for complacency. We must try to identify and publicise any current examples of good practice and, at the same time, we must explore feasible strategies for the future.

Good practice is only the litmus paper test of a harmonious fit between appropriate values, explicit strategic objectives based on those values, and effective implementation strategies for achieving those objectives. The Family Support Network, based at the Universities of Keele and East Anglia, provides a practical means of exchanging information about policy and practice developments.

The latest child abuse research studies[4] have offered an opportunity, the first for over a decade, to carefully, constructively and innovatively devise and deliver both a family support *and* a child protection service. The tide in recent years has been forceful and one-directional, in some cases towards ever more heavy-handed and oppressive investigations, leaving many children and families no better off. Some are probably measurably worse off and the system itself is an expensive one, threatening any or even equal financial allocation to 'family support work'.

If real change is to take place, then some conditions have to be met and some practical structures put in place. There are five distinct but inter-dependent aspects to this.

1. *The Government needs to lead from the front*

   While the Government is not solely responsible for the direction of our child care services, its lead is vital. It is disingenuous to suggest, as the Minister did at the launch of the research overview, that the view that many Section 47 investigations are a waste of time is 'not the message we want to send'. 'Too many investigations' is an eminently reasonable interpretation of the research findings and one that will have to be acknowledged if the public, and the families involved, are to have any belief that there is a commitment to change.

The Government should recognise that front-line workers do need protection, but not through heavy-handed relations with families, inevitably caused by consciousness of the establishment and the media on their backs. Ministers and the public should accept that no system is risk free. They should provide protection through positive encouragement towards a new style, albeit also with risks, that is accepted by the Government, the media and the community at large.

Ministers must encourage local authorities to raise their thresholds for child protection interventions. That is the first requirement if the fishing net is to stop catching the minnows.

But social services cannot do the job alone. They are not big enough, in as much as families clearly state that the services they want come from a range of agencies. Section 27 was meant to bring this about, as it enables local authorities to call on other authorities and persons for help in the exercise of their functions and obliges those authorities to comply 'if it is compatible with their own statutory and other duties and obligations and does not unduly prejudice the discharge of any of their functions'. But other agencies use its get-out clause all too frequently. This loophole needs closing. Not only would that create an actual change, but it would also send the kind of direct message that is so badly needed.

Finally, the Government needs to consider the current role of the Area Child Protection Committee (ACPC) as the only formal multi-agency planning forum. It has been effective within its narrow definition of child protection, but is not the right forum to deal with family support and an integrated model of practice and policy. What is needed is a new forum, with the same if not greater status, whose primary focus is on meeting children's needs through family support. Ideally child protection issues would be embraced within this as one of a number of important sub-groups. The work being done by the Department of Health on local authorities' Children's Services Plans[5] is one promising structure which could be developed to accommodate such a forum.

2. *Social services departments need to lead from the top*
With so much time and resources currently being committed to the child

protection system, the professionals with lead responsibility may react defensively to the research messages. Those at the top can show the way by avoiding defensiveness, by acknowledging that good practice develops and accepts change, and by not asking us to go at a snail's pace when we have enough knowledge to begin to make changes now. Some local authorities have started by concentrating on what can be done and by confronting reluctant professional attitudes. They have done this within their own resources, and often in areas of enormous deprivation. They show that commitment is every bit as important as resources and that, given the right internal structures, resources can be reallocated with considerable speed.

Just as the Government needs to give a clear lead in raising the threshold for referrals, so too do local authorities and ACPCs. We should see encouragement for referrals to be made about and for children not as child protection services but as children in need of family support services. We should see a more positive response to families who ask for help. We should plan for the day when other professionals no longer say that the only way they can hope to get even a support-type service for a family is to make a Section 47 referral requiring a full investigation. A lighter touch in response to Section 47 referrals is required: there is a valid distinction to be made between investigations and inquiries. Alongside that, a ratio of more Section 17 referrals and fewer Section 47 referrals would be appropriate and effective. Implicit within such a redirection is the provision of protection for the front-line workers when something goes wrong.

If family support services are to develop appropriately and effectively, professionals will have to believe that this is the work they want to do. This work is an area of professional activity long overdue for improved status, possibly even the elite status that now attaches to child protection specialisms. The professional culture has to change. Family support should be treated as a specialism in itself, and not something intuitive. Local authorities need to award it this status in terms of staff, time and practical resources.

All this can happen if the professionals tackle the issues seriously. It cannot wholly succeed, however, if undertaken by professionals alone, without an active partnership with the community and service users.

The child abuse researchers did talk to families with a resulting impact on the outcomes of the studies.[6,7,8,9] Families have a continuing and unique role to play. They should be invited in at the beginning, and thereafter, to join the debate in every local authority, to sit on planning groups, to take part in planning family support services and structures, and to take part long term in their monitoring and evaluation. Their participation must not be left as a paper recognition in the research studies. Rather these studies could be seen as a valuable example of how to make the most of everyone's expertise.

3. *Front-line staff need to see families as an opportunity and not as a threat to their children*
Even if all the above changes were to take place, the front-line professionals remain the crucial link to service-user experience. The Children Act's push for partnership with families still waits to be fully realised. Families are entitled to a generous welcome, not to suspicion. Their efforts to secure what they need for their families should be seen as a sign of their commitment, not as a sign of their failure.

All who have responsibility for raising children feel burdened by the messages about how easily families can damage them and about the extent of their needs which families feel inadequate to meet. When they ask for help they need their wavering confidence and rapidly diminishing self-esteem building up, not further reduced. They need the professionals to see that they care, that they want to do well for their children and that they don't find it easy to ask for help.

Families constantly say that they are undermined rather than empowered. Yet professionals say that they want to empower families. What goes wrong? What can be done? Families talk freely about good experiences and their list of what helps is brief and deceptively simple: give us good written information at the beginning; keep us regularly informed about what is happening and what could happen; make sure that we have access to good advocacy; be genuinely interested in what we see as the problem and how we think we could be helped, whether we are adults or young people; treat us with respect; make sure that you really have taken account of our views and in such a way that we are in no doubt about that; and provide an effective complaints procedure.

These are not new ideas, but they deserve a fresh look at how they could be realised.

4. *Other agencies need to play a larger role*
Social services neither can, nor should, do everything alone. Many other professionals and families themselves testify to this. Many families would be better assisted by the provision of services from voluntary agencies, from a broader provision within health services and from more wide-ranging services provided within their children's schools.

For instance, narrow definitions of a school's community role miss a vital opportunity to reach families in a familiar setting before problems get out of hand. Primary school teaching staff are unnerved by the worries and distress they see in families but which they feel they have neither the time, nor sometimes the skill, to respond to helpfully. So, eyes are closed or child protection referrals made. Pastoral care for families which can reach those who want it, and possibly a greater role for school nurses, should be back on the agenda. This has been achieved in some schools through joint co-ordinating strategies held under the umbrella of Children's Services Plans and through inter-departmental and agency funding.

5. *Recognition that family support is not just a service but is also a concept and a style of delivery*
Families say that when they go for help, they get nothing or they get investigated. They don't get asked what they want but rather get assessed, diagnosed, pathologised and then get handed a decision about what is to be done. Being provided with family support services in this context is experienced as an imposition and a threat, not as a support.

This may explain the gulf between some workers saying they do more family support than child protection work and those very same families saying they don't get family support services. What they don't get is the service they believe they need, within a style of decision making and delivery which they find supportive. Family Group Conferences have begun to make an important contribution to creating a family-friendly style of decision making.[10,11] Only by professionals talking to families both about what services they want and how they want them delivered can this gaping hole be plugged. Talking and working together does achieve more than either can alone. If we have both the services and the style right, then we have a genuine chance of matching hopes with outcomes. To do this, service users need to be involved in the debate about style and services.

When the Department of Health recently asked a group of families involved in child protection investigations what sort of family support services they would like,[12] their list included: financial assistance for them to purchase individualised help packages; practical services in their home; advocacy services; counselling help, especially for their children, after traumatic events, including investigations which do not result in registration; a view of the family as valuable in its own right, and to be given services as a family; an early response to their requests for help; and open door family centres providing a range of services to the local community.

Interestingly, many of these are already in existence. We could build on those which work, examine why some others seem to miss the mark, and develop more.

### Values and philosophy

The following four principles indicate wider values which underpin the notion of partnership in work with children and their families. They are all derived from the Government's published material on principles and practice in child care work.[13,14]

- *Universalism* We all use and need services, whether we are managing to lead relatively normal lives or are in crisis under stress.
- *Equality and equity of access to services* Everyone in our community has rights to accessible support services.
- *The normality of difficulties in parenting* Services should support and supplement families' endeavours.
- *Participation* Parents usually know what their needs are and their views should be taken seriously.

## Strategic objectives

The following five objectives have been identified as appropriate to the requirements of the new legislation:[15]

1. Services should be provided across the local and health authorities rather than being confined to social services departments, and they should involve the voluntary and private sectors.
2. A programme should be established for assessing needs and monitoring unmet needs.
3. A continuum of support services for families should be developed, so that packages can be offered flexibly in response to a diverse range of needs. Statutory, private and voluntary services should be used.
4. Mechanisms should be developed for involving and representing the needs and wishes of children, parents and their wider kinship/community networks.
5. Services should be published, and systems identified to do this.

## Implementation strategies

There are countrywide examples of local authorities who have shown that it is possible to attempt most or at least some of these challenges and who have tried to avoid treating partnership as a moveable feast or as a matter of expediency. Where family support and any other child care objectives are concerned, partnership should be an integrated element of the *policy* and *process*, as well as part of *practice* itself. In fact, one of the valuable characteristics of the 1989 Act is the novel extent to which it explicitly addresses planning and policy. In order to emphasise this aspect, as well as to provide training and material for officers, a significant attempt was made before October 1991 to involve elected representatives. The Department of Health commissioned special material as part of this strategy.[16]

Newcastle Social Services Department has set up a local planning system that is intended to allow reasonable debate between users and providers. Their policy statement[17] talks of a 'planning structure and process which produces locally co-ordinated services which have community consent and are accessible and non-stigmatising'. The notion of community consent, or a community mandate, is as crucial at the family support end of the child care spectrum as it is at the explicit child protection end of it.

Many readers will be familiar with the Mack and Lansley report[18] about 'breadline Britain' where citizens were asked what they regarded as essential resources for an individual to have in order to avoid the description of being in poverty or hardship. Such an approach, with the aim of drawing a community picture of normative aims and aspirations, is just as relevant to child care issues. Waltham Forest Social Services Department went into schools and asked children in the community what they wanted from the 1989 Act.[19] Social work often appears to concentrate so much on what is problematic and abnormal that, where plans for family support are concerned, it is even more important to cast the net of consultation as widely as possible into the community.

The assessment of need is a very large part of both the Children Act and the NHS and Community Care Act. It, too, has emerged from the long night of unilateral professional control into, at least theoretically, a process in which users and providers will collaborate. There is a two-fold assessment process to be accomplished: on the one hand, the ascertaining of need "in the area" and, on the other, the assessment of "individual" need. Partnership requires that potential users are involved in both aspects, in contributing to an area-wide picture of need as well as participating actively in the assessment of their own eligibility for a particular service to meet their needs. The most imaginative local authorities have explored new ways of doing both these things, and in some cases it has involved drawing on the particular strengths and skills of a voluntary organisation.

The Children's Society has working agreements in several aspects.[20] At the "area" end of the spectrum, they have produced a computer package which can be used by projects like a family centre to undertake, for example, a survey of child/family needs on a particular estate. At the "individual" need end of the spectrum, their family centre in Newport, Wales might, for example, draw up an agreement with the local authority and family to find out the wants and needs of the family, and the wishes and views of the local authority, and then work as an advocate for the family.

Family Service Units have a written Clients' Rights Policy,[21] which both informs the way the unit works as an organisation and prompts the local authorities with whom it makes service agreements or contracts. The elements in this policy include:

- the right to high-quality service across the whole spectrum of organisational facilities including training, recording, decision making and management;

- the prioritisation of anti-discriminatory issues;
- the provision of interpretation and translation facilities where appropriate;
- the availability of a social policy worker to enable service users in groups to speak out on issues that affect them.

## Comment

There are many diverse ways in which users can participate in planning for family support policies, in influencing the systems which deliver them, and in contributing to the mechanisms which ensure high-quality service delivery. The intention of the Children Act 1989 that users should participate in this way is clear, and no political, professional or administrative audience should assume that it fails to apply to them.

The challenge for local authority social services departments is to facilitate that participation in a variety of ways, of which the above examples are only suggestions. For researchers, there is a clear duty to ensure that the user's perspective is incorporated into their methodology. For politicians, there is a democratic imperative to listen to what their constituents want, and not be influenced only by the most affluent or those who shout the loudest. For all of us, there is a need to affirm the importance of participation, and to accept the notion that we all might, at one time in our lives, be a member of *any* client/user grouping. Food for thought!

## References

1 Marsh P, and Fisher M, *Good Intentions: Developing partnerships in social services*, Community Care into Practice series, Joseph Rowntree Foundation, 1992.

2 Thoburn J (ed), *Participation in Practice – Involving families in child protection*, Department of Health/University of East Anglia, 1992.

3 Aldgate J, and Tunstill J, *Implementing Section 17 of the Children Act 1989*, HMSO, 1996.

4 Department of Health, *Child Protection: Messages from research*, HMSO, 1995.

5   Sutton P, *Crossing the Boundaries: A discussion of children's services plans*, National Children's Bureau, 1995. Also Social Services Inspectorate, *Children's Services Plans: An analysis of children's services plans 1993/94*, Department of Health, 1995.

6   Farmer E, and Owen M, *Child Protection Practice: Private risks and public remedies*, HMSO, 1995.

7   Gibbons J, Gallagher B, Bell C, and Gordon D, *Development After Physical Abuse in Early Childhood: A follow-up study of children on protection registers*, HMSO, 1995.

8   Cleaver H, and Freeman P, *Parental Perspectives in Cases of Suspected Child Abuse*, HMSO, 1995.

9   Thoburn J, Lewis A, and Shemmings D, *Paternalism or Partnership: Family involvement in the child protection process*, HMSO, 1995.

10  Morris K, *Family Group Conferences: An introductory pack*, Family Rights Group, 1995.

11  Morris K, and Tunnard J (eds), *Family Group Conferences: Messages from UK practice and research*, Family Rights Group, 1996.

12  Unpublished papers of a consultation day with families at the Department of Health in June 1995. This was the second consultation day held as part of the work involved in producing: Department of Health/Social Services Inspectorate, *The Challenge of Partnership in Child Protection: Practice guide*, HMSO, 1995.

13  Department of Health, *The Care of Children: Principles and practice in regulations and guidance*, HMSO, 1989.

14  Children In Need Implementation Group, *The Children Act and Children's Needs: Make it the answer and not the problem*, National Council of Voluntary Child Care Organisations and Family Rights Group, 1991.

15  See 14 above.

16  Brocklesby E, Masson J, and Shaw M, *Children in Need and their Families: A new approach, A manual for Senior Managers on Part III of the Children Act 1989*, The University of Leicester School of Social Work and Faculty of Law and the Department of Health, 1991.

17   *Children's Services Plan 1*, Newcastle Social Services, Civic Centre, Newcastle upon Tyne, NE1 8PA.

18   Mack J, and Lansley S, *Breadline Britain in the 1990s*, Harper Collins, 1992.

19   Unpublished internal report.

20   The Children's Society, Edward Rudolf House, Margery Street, London WC1 has *Working Agreements with Clients*.

21   Family Services Unit, 207 Old Marylebone Road, London N1 has a *written Clients' Rights Policy*.

# 5   The paediatric role: providing assessment, treatment and continuity

*Margaret A Lynch*

*Dr Margaret A Lynch is a Reader in Community Paediatrics, at United Medical and Dental Schools of Guy's and St Thomas' Hospitals, University of London. She is also Medical Director of Optimum Health Services NHS Trust.*

**Once a paediatrician has made an assessment of an abused child, many problems lie ahead. Who will make sure the child gets all the help needed to assure emotional and mental, as well as physical development? This chapter examines the role the paediatrician and other medical and paramedical professionals can play in the planning and provision of therapeutic services to children and families who have come to notice during a child protection investigation or assessment.**

The provision of comprehensive co-ordinated care with continuity of follow up for children and families who have come to notice during a child protection investigation or assessment has never been easy and is likely to be further challenged by the effects of recent social policy trends and health and social service "reforms".[1] Effective intervention plans are dependent on identification of need followed by referral to a service with the expertise and capacity to respond in an appropriate way.

Gaining the full co-operation of not only the child and family but also of other professionals and, when appropriate, foster carers, is very important. Even then, intervention needed to promote the child's development may be overshadowed by other demands on the carer's or even the child's time. Waiting lists and differences in the way in which services are delivered and costed will influence an individual child's access to assessment and treatment. These factors are likely to cause most problems for the child in a temporary placement.

Because of the continuing preoccupation with sexual abuse, resources and attention can be diverted away from identifying and meeting the often diffuse and long-term needs of physically abused and neglected children.

### Defining the paediatrician's role

All too often the paediatric contribution is perceived both within and outside the profession as being restricted to either the recognition of signs of physical abuse/or the physical examination of children where abuse is suspected. Both these circumstances will be covered by local Area Child Protection Committee procedures with which the paediatrician is expected to be (but may not be) familiar. Paediatricians concerned that a child is being or has been abused should share such concerns with social services. Many are reluctant to do this. Some avoid examination of children when the possibility of abuse has already been recognised. Where senior paediatricians avoid involvement, junior staff will not receive the necessary training or support. Left feeling uncertain of their role, junior paediatricians are likely to resolve their inevitable anxiety by themselves learning avoidance techniques. Indeed, the opinion is being voiced within the profession that recruitment is being adversely affected by fear of involvement in "child protection".

Because of the emphasis on the paediatrician's role in the initial investigation of suspected abuse and neglect, a potential wider role has been largely ignored. Repeated studies of abused and neglected children[2,3,4] have shown them to have problems of unmet health needs, and problems of growth and development. In a recent study by Thoburn et al[5] on family participation in child protection, just under half of the children were recognised by the case conference to have health, emotional, or behavioural problems or learning disabilities.

By shifting the emphasis on the paediatric involvement away from the investigation to advising on the overall medical care of the child, the expertise of paediatricians would be used more appropriately. This approach is in line with the philosophy of the Children Act 1989. It should make it more likely that the medical and developmental needs of the child are met, so positively influencing the long-term outcome for both child and family. Nonetheless, paediatricians will still have to contribute to the initial recognition and investigation of suspected child abuse and neglect and, in a few cases, give evidence in court to ensure the child's protection. Participation in these activities should be seen as an integral part of paediatricians' responsibility to their patients.

With the increasing trend for child health surveillance to be undertaken by general practitioners or their attached health visitors, Primary Health Care teams should become more involved in child protection. The paediatrician will have an important role in contributing to the planning and providing of any necessary local training, and ensuring that experienced staff are available to provide family doctors and health visitors with advice and support.

## Recognition of need

The examination of a child following an allegation of abuse or with a possible non-accidental injury should be more than a quest for forensic evidence and a full medical history should be obtained. The medical examination should be a thorough one, not just focusing on injuries and other overt evidence of recent abuse. Routine health needs of children who are abused and neglected, or who come from families under stress, may well have been overlooked by their parents and professionals already involved with the family. Such needs include immunisations, the monitoring of growth and development, and dental checks. The child protection medical should be seen as an opportunity to identify any action that needs to be taken to ensure immunisations and screening are up to date. If evidence of acute or chronic ill health is found, appropriate investigations and treatment should be organised and arrangements for follow-up made. This should be offered regardless of the outcome of the abuse investigation.

Under the Children Act, "significant harm" is considered to have occurred if maltreatment can be demonstrated, or if it can be shown that the child's health or development is being impaired. Even if maltreatment can be clearly demonstrated by describing injuries diagnostic of physical abuse or by demonstrating grossly distorted parent-child interactions, attention must be given to all aspects of the child's health and development.[6] If the emphasis is merely to get enough evidence to obtain a court order, the wider implications for the child's long term development may be overlooked.

As part of an assessment following the identification of abuse or neglect

53

of a child, full assessments of the health and development of all the children in the family should take place. Support should be offered to the parents to enable them to keep appointments, whether or not further action is to be taken in relation to the suspected maltreatment.

Whenever a child at risk is seen for any medical examination, such as a school medical or a statutory medical for children in care or accommodation, the opportunity should be taken to review all aspects of the child's health, growth and development. These dimensions should likewise be considered for all children in the family at review case conferences. These reviews should be seen as opportunities for monitoring already known problems and identifying new or previously unrecognised ones.

If, as usually currently happens with child sexual abuse, the demands of the criminal justice system are allowed to dominate the agenda, the paediatrician may find it even more difficult to play a therapeutic role. Yet the paediatrician remains the best equipped professional to examine and assess the child. Many sexually abused children have a combination of medical, psychosomatic and developmental problems which need recognition, investigation, appropriate treatment and follow-up. In a recent study by Prior et al,[7] children were asked for their views on the investigative process. They clearly indicated they wanted explanations and information, including the results of the medical examination and investigations. Paediatricians should be able to provide this in a way that is appropriate to the child's developmental level.

**Referral and provision of services**
Once a child has been recognised as having a medical or developmental problem which requires intervention, a referral must be made to a service capable of responding in an appropriate way. For the majority of children, the further investigations and treatment facilities are available within mainstream services, but families may need support and encouragement to use them. Those providing the services must be prepared to appreciate the special needs of abused children and their families, and be willing to modify their style of practice, when necessary. For example, service providers should try to ensure that early appointments are not given to families who 'have trouble getting going in the mornings'. They should also be flexible

about the place in which the child is seen: community settings are often less stressful for all concerned. If an opinion from a consultant in another speciality is needed, a joint appointment with the doctor already known by the family often makes the encounter more effective and easier for parents and child. Only if services are willing to adapt will children be ensured equality of access. This is likely to be facilitated if the paediatrician making the initial assessment remains involved in the child's ongoing care.

Following the identification of abuse or neglect, the assessments of the child's health and development should be used to inform the child protection plan. This should include appropriate medical intervention and, for the child with developmental problems, access to a child development team and appropriate treatment. Research and clinical experiences indicate that the speech and language therapist is most likely to be in demand,[8] yet few services have the resources to enable them to respond appropriately to the needs of these children and their carers. This is particularly difficult for children who move because, after each move, the child is likely to require a new referral and be placed at the bottom of the new locality's waiting list. This may well mean the child is never seen for therapy.

The assessment should also identify children who need referral to child mental health services for further assessment and possible therapy because of behavioural problems or emotional difficulties. Once again, pressures on the child mental health services mean that there are often long waits for children to be seen which can understandably undermine a parent's motivation to co-operate with therapeutic plans.

When a child is thought to be suffering "significant harm" because of impairment of health and/or development, the assessment must look beyond proving that harm has occurred. Consideration must be given to the investigation, treatment and follow-up of any problems identified. This is easier when the paediatrician undertaking the assessment is locally based with access to diagnostic facilities and the expertise of a child development team. There is more danger of not meeting the child's health and developmental needs if an assessment is undertaken by an "expert" from outside the area, and information not be shared with those responsible for the local child health services. It is essential to address health and development whether or not any court action results in the granting of an order. The results and implications of the assessment must be carefully explained to all those involved in the care of the child and taken into consideration when making future plans for the child and family. The family doctor, health visitor and, for the older child, the school health service all need to be aware of any special needs the child may have, any referrals made, and any intervention recommended. The paediatrician cannot rely on information filtering through via case conference minutes.

For the child in foster care, the provision of medical and child development services presents particular difficulties, and these are likely to be exacerbated by the health service reforms. Routine primary health care will transfer temporarily to the general practitioner used by the carers who is unlikely to have information on the child's medical history unless someone has assumed responsibility for passing this on. Transfer of notes between family doctors can take weeks and will not take place at all if the child is registered as a temporary resident. Parent-held records should in theory overcome some of these problems, but in practice may not be up to date unless the parents have taken them to all medical consultations and the doctors have made an entry, something many are not willing to do. Frequently, too, when a child is being removed from home, the atmosphere is such that remembering to ask for the parent-held records is easily forgotten, or the parents cannot find them or are reluctant to hand them over. There are occasions where the failure to share medical information could have serious, even life threatening, consequences for a child. The following case illustrates this.

*Case*

    Two sisters were placed in a foster home following the psychiatric breakdown of their mother. While hospitalised, she was diagnosed as having malignant hyperpyrexia (a potentially fatal extreme rise in body temperature in response to certain drugs including commonly used anaesthetics). This condition is familial, putting the girls at risk. The local hospital and GP notes were marked and information about the condition shared in writing with social services. Rehabilitation with the mother became impossible and the sisters were moved to a small therapeutic children's home in another part of the country. It is unclear what information about the girls' medical history was given to the care staff. Certainly the new GP received no medical reports. Only after he had referred one of the sisters for consideration for minor ENT surgery did one of the care staff remember a vague warning over the danger of anaesthetic. The GP only obtained the full history after he had taken the trouble to track down the paediatrician who had previously known the children. She had not been told the children had moved. Both doctors were justifiably angry that failure of effective communication had put a child's life at risk.

While this is an example of a rare condition, there are more common disorders, such as sickle cell disease, the symptoms of which need prompt recognition and treatment if death is to be avoided.

Many of the medical and developmental needs of abused and neglected children are diffuse, not necessarily easily definable at first, and often likely to be long term. For many of the children, both positive and negative effects of environmental changes on their development will not become apparent without careful follow-up by the same child development team.

Continuity is particularly important for the child who is failing to thrive. Both height and weight need accurate monitoring, preferably by the same person using the same equipment and at intervals appropriate to the child's age. Changes in the child's rate of growth may well relate to changes in the child's or family's circumstances. If intervention is meeting the child's physical and psychological needs, this should be reflected in improved growth. However, it must not be forgotten that abused and neglected children may occasionally have an organic reason for their growth failure. Paediatricians should be alert to this possibility during investigation and advise on appropriate investigation.

There are children known to paediatricians because of medical problems or disability identified before child protection issues are raised. For these children, and for those identified as part of a child abuse evaluation as having major medical problems, the paediatrician will have a key role. All those involved in the child's care and planning for the future, including courts, must be aware of the implications of a disability or medical condition and take it into consideration when advising parents. If the child is placed away from the birth parents, access to appropriate specialist care must be considered when selecting a placement. When a placement is short term, it may be better for the paediatrician who is familiar with and to the child to continue follow-up, even if this requires some travelling by the foster carer or the paediatrician. Provision of such continuity has not always been seen as a priority by either paediatricians or social workers. In the future continuity may become even more difficult to organise unless funding is allowed for such an eventuality within Provider's contracts.

Because investigation of child sexual abuse is currently driven by the needs of the criminal justice system, the paediatrician may find it difficult to ensure that the welfare of the child is always put first. The expertise and sensitivity shown by many police child protection teams[9] in the initial investigation may well appear to put the best interests of the child first. Only later do the conflicts between the child's needs and requirements of the criminal justice system become apparent. For example, the lawyers may want a second medical opinion, including further examination of the child, not for medical but for evidential reasons. The wider assessment of the effects on the child and the referral for psychotherapeutic help is still positively discouraged by many Crown Prosecution Service lawyers until after the trial. This is to avoid the defence claiming the child's evidence has been contaminated.[10] Prior et al[11] found that, by the time the trial is over or, as is more likely, the criminal proceedings have been dropped as most cases never get to court, the child and family may be so disillusioned with "justice", that they refuse any services offered. The child, moreover, is in danger of developing life-long feelings of hostility and distrust towards both social and health services. Paediatricians may see themselves as advocates on behalf of the child, advising against further, medically unjustified examinations. They can point out that Department of Health (DoH) guidance clearly puts the therapeutic needs of the child above those of the criminal justice system.[12] At times it will be appropriate to refer for therapy regardless of the view of the actual or hypothetical prosecution barrister.

## Consent and co-operation

The undertaking of appropriate assessments and the subsequent attendance for treatment and follow-up therapy will be dependent on the consent of those with parental responsibility. Under the Children Act, this responsibility may be shared by parents not living together or by a local authority and parent(s). Children of sufficient understanding are also in a position to give their own consent. If necessary, a parent's refusal can be challenged using provisions within the Children Act.

For any treatment programme to succeed, it is necessary to gain the co-operation both of those involved with a child's care and the child. Birth parents may be unwilling or unable to follow through on a treatment programme or keep follow-up medical appointments. Given the chaos their lives may be in, and the demands on their time once social services have become involved, it is easy to understand why a speech therapy appoint-ment is not seen as a priority, particularly as the child may have been on the waiting list for months. If an appointment is missed, another may not be offered as a technique by some overstretched services to control case loads and waiting lists. Services under great pressure may also remove those with high non-attendance rates as a way to meet targets demanded by contracts and based on the number of client contacts and waiting times. This discriminates not just against chronically disorganised families but also those disrupted by crises such as parental illness or bereavement.

To ensure the maximum uptake of mainstream services by families with children who have been abused or neglected, it is important to help the parents, and where appropriate the child, understand why the treatment and follow-up are necessary, and why it may need to be by a particular clinician in a given clinic. Those providing and managing the service must be prepared to recognise the special needs of such children and families and be prepared to meet them in a flexible way. Others involved with the family, including social workers and the courts, also need to be aware of the treatment needs of the child. They should be prepared to encourage and support parents to facilitate attendance. Some arrangements for assessment of parents, access and rehabilitation are so complicated that there is little time available to consider a child's medical and treatment needs. The following case illustrates this.

## Case

A three-year-old girl with developmental delay and little language was in foster care while an assessment of her father's parenting skills took place with a view to their rehabilitation. In addition to her attendance at a family centre with her father, the little girl's week also included separate access visits by her mother and grandmother, a full diary for a three-year-old! Any appointments for developmental assessment or speech therapy had to be fitted around these commitments. Consequently, appointments would be cancelled or not kept if, for example, the time of an access visit was changed or if the appointment coincided with a court hearing. The time spent at the family centre was seen as assessing the father's abilities rather than promoting the child's development. The recommended nursery school place could not be taken up because of the child's other commitments. Work with the child's developmental problems could only start once the child was living full time with her father. Understandably, by then he took some convincing by the child development team that this was necessary.

When a child is living in a foster home, in addition to the demands of access visits to or by birth parents, the commitments of the foster carers and the needs of other children in the household have to be taken into account when trying to preserve continuity of treatment and follow up.

**Prevention of child abuse and neglect**
While this paper has focused on the paediatrician's role in the identification and treatment of the health and developmental needs of abused and neglected children, this has been in the context of tertiary prevention: the provision of services to prevent recurrence. For the child killed or disabled by the abuse such intervention comes too late. There is also considerable evidence that tertiary prevention does not even work well for many of the survivors. Physical abuse can recur in at least half of all cases referred to child protection agencies[13] and sexual abuse will recur in the majority of cases where the offender remains in the family.[14] Thus it seems appropriate to conclude a paper on the therapeutic option with some consideration of the paediatrician's role in primary and secondary prevention.

Primary prevention is essentially the promotion of the well-being of all children and families. Thus any reform or innovation that improves the living standards of the majority of the population is likely to contribute to the prevention of child maltreatment. Arguably more realistic and potentially more effective are commitments to influence attitudes towards children and to provide education on child rearing. Paediatricians working in partnership with communities have an obvious role to play here. Their involvement with individual families and children, for example, in child health surveillance clinics, provides opportunities to ensure parents have the necessary support and skills to rear their children. Parents need to feel confident that their paediatrician is interested in all aspects of their child's development including their own interactions with and enjoyment of the child.

It is perhaps in secondary prevention that the paediatrician has the most important and rewarding role to play. Secondary prevention can be summarised as the identification of high risk groups, followed by ensuring the use of existing resources, and when necessary supplying additional services, aimed at preventing abuse. Paediatricians are usually aware of factors that make some children more vulnerable within a community, or even within a family, already known to them.

Early studies in the United Kingdom by Lynch[15] and Lynch et al[16] showed that children born prematurely, sick or disabled, born different or unwanted, are at increased risk of abuse and/or neglect. Some of these are babies where the paediatrician has an early opportunity of gaining the parents' trust and encouraging them to work as partners with the professionals. The paediatrician may also be able to identify factors that make the parents more vulnerable in their own right.[17] All too often, vulnerable parents produce a vulnerable baby, increasing further the risk of maltreatment. Parents who were abused and neglected in their own childhood are known to experience great difficulties in child rearing.[18] Some may turn to the paediatrician from their childhood for support. All should be seen as a target group for additional help and advice. Other factors that have been identified as contributing to child abuse include domestic violence[19] and relationship problems; psychological and physical ill health; early parenthood; loss of a previous baby; multiple social problems and isolation with little or no family or community support.[20,21] The paediatrician can encourage such families to use any existing mainstream health and social facilities.

Some families will require referral to specialist resources, so the paediatrician needs to know in some detail about local facilities including those run by voluntary groups. Vulnerable families may initially resist participation or passively accept anything on offer. The challenge is to engage them as true partners in the care of their children.

# References

1 Lynch M A, 'Child Protection: Have we lost our way?' *Adoption & Fostering*, 16:4, 15–22, BAAF, 1992.

2 Lynch M A, Roberts J, *Consequences of Child Abuse*, Academic Press, 1982.

3 Augoustinos M, 'Developmental Effects of Child Abuse: Recent Findings', *Child Abuse and Neglect*, 11:15–27, 1987.

4 Lynch M A, 'The consequences of child abuse', in Browne K, Davies C, Stratton P (eds), *Early Prediction and Prevention of Child Abuse*, John Wiley and Sons, 1988.

5 Thoburn J, Lewis A, Shemmings D, 'Family Participation in Child Protection', *Child Abuse Review*, 4, in press, 1995.

6 Lynch M A, 'Significant Harm: The Paediatric Contribution', in White R, Adcock M, Hollows A (eds), *Significant Harm*, Significant Publications, 1991.

7 Prior V, Lynch M, and Glaser D, *Messages from Children: Children's evaluations of the professional response to child sexual abuse*, NCH Action For Children, 1994.

8 Law J, Conway J, 'Effect of Abuse and Neglect on the Development of Children's Speech and Language', *Developmental Medicine and Child Neurology*, 34:943–948, 1992.

9 See 7 above.

10 Joel-Esam B, 'Preventing Child Abuse in the Courtroom: Evidence on Commission', *Child Abuse Review*, 3:231–233, 1994.

11 See 7 above.

12 Department of Health, *Working Together*, HMSO, 1991.

13 Magura M, 'Are Services to Protect Children Effective?', *Children and Youth Service Review*, 3:193, 1981.

14 Bentovim A, 'Clinical work with Families in which Sexual Abuse has Occurred', in Hollin C, and Howells K (eds), *Clinical Approaches to Sex Offenders and their Victims*, John Wiley and Sons, 1991.

15 Lynch M A, 'Ill health and Child Abuse', *Lancet*, 2:317–319, 1975.

16 Lynch M A, Roberts J, Gordon M, 'Child Abuse: Early warnings in the Maternity Hospital', *Developmental Medicine and Child Neurology*, 1976.

17 Roberts J, 'Why are Some Families More Vulnerable to Child Abuse?', in Browne K, Davies C, Stratton P (eds), *Early Prediction and Prevention of Child Abuse*, John Wiley and Sons, 1988.

18 Bowlby J, 'The Making and Breaking of Affectional Bonds', *British Journal of Psychiatry*, 130, 1977.

19 Browne K D, 'Violence in the Family and its Links to Child Abuse', in Hobbs C J, Wynne J M (eds), *Clinical Paediatrics: Child Abuse*, Bailliere Tindall, 1993.

20 See 17 above.

21 Lynch M A, Roberts J, 'Predicting Child Abuse: Signs of bonding failure in the maternity hospital', *British Medical Journal*, 1:624–626, 1977.

# 6 Understanding the child
## The importance of thinking about the child's feelings

*Judith Trowell*

*Dr Judith Trowell is a Consultant Child and Adolescent Psychiatrist at the Tavistock Clinic. She is also an Honorary Senior Lecturer at the Royal Free Hospital School of Medicine, and the Chairperson of Young Minds.*

**How can professionals resolve conflicts between the needs and feelings of children and the responsibilities of adults in the complex situations of abused children and their families? The author outlines factors that are important in understanding children and how their feelings may conflict with those of adults whose duty is to protect them. She makes a case for careful assessment of all viewpoints, bearing in mind that the ultimate responsibility for decisions lies with the adults.**

In all complex situations there are conflicting needs, rights and views, and the effects of the process can largely depend on finding the right balance between these conflicts. The initial conflict frequently concerns children's rights and children's needs. Children have a right to give consent and to have a say in what happens to them, including interviews and investigations, but adults have the responsibility to ensure that children's needs are met.

Where children need protection and where their physical, emotional, psychological and social development is in question, adults may have very different views from the child. For example, in a sexually abusive relationship between a child and adult carer, the child may wish to keep the family intact rather than face a possible break up if the abuse is stopped. I was very shaken when an 11-year-old girl in foster care told me she hated what her dad did to her (vaginal and anal intercourse) and wanted it to stop, but she did not want her dad to be put in prison, nor for her, her sister and her brother to stay in foster care. What she wanted more than anything was to be back as a family. Foster care was worse than living at home as a family, with the abuse, but as a family.

Society has agreed a minimum level of care for children and the United Kingdom has signed the UN Declaration on the Rights of the Child. While we seem to have some agreement on what children need, we have not adequately considered children's rights given this consensus. At what age can a child refuse to be interviewed? Or decline investigation? Or state who they want to parent them? The Children Act 1989 and the Gillick ruling[1] have gone some way to meet this, but much confusion and uncertainty remains.

This links in with another area of conflict. Caring for children consists of the constant struggle to find a balance between the use of authority and the need to show care and concern. The capacity to say no in the child's best interest, and the capacity to love, that is, show affection and commitment are not easy when the child wants something we believe is damaging (like the girl mentioned earlier who was begging to go back to an abusive home).

### The professional's role

Professionals need to use authority and show concern, and this must under-pin all their decisions. They have their own conflicts about what they are doing alongside those of the child and the parents. In order for the process to be conducted in a way that respects the child and at the same time retains adult responsibility, the work must be done by professionals who have a good knowledge base, observational skills, an awareness of child development and communication skills. The whole child must be understood, including the body and physical needs, the mind and psychological development, the feelings and emotional development, and the spirit and creativity. By creativity I mean the child's capacity to be aware of and in touch with an aspect of our humanity that links with music, art, literature, and the imagination. It means playing with ideas, becoming aware of the longing for immortality; it is something outside our own experience, a rainbow, a spider's web covered in raindrops or frost.

In order to accomplish this, the professional needs to keep in mind a range of theoretical frameworks. These concern the child's internal development, psychodynamic theory and attachment, the child's family constellation, systems theory, and the family context. Issues of race, gender, culture, class and disability are important in this regard. The process can be very destructive if these issues are not recognised and given due weight. Children's ascertainable wishes and feelings can only be understood if they themselves are fully understood. However, in each case, the child's best interests are paramount. So the outcome may not be the one the child wanted but the one the responsible adults agreed was best. To help understand the whole child, there are many factors the professional needs to consider. The figures on the following page illustrate some of the major ones.

### The world of the child

*The parent's role*

An additional complexity is how to determine what is good enough parenting. What are parental responsibilities, for example, when the effects of the process on the child can be linked to the parental response? Browne et al[2] have shown that, in sexually abused children, the traumatic effect of the abuse is strongly linked to the parental response on its disclosure rather than to the nature and extent of the abuse itself.

What do we mean by parental responsibility? Parents need to meet a child's physical, emotional, psychological and social needs. If physical care is adequate, then the parent's commitment to the child and the capacity to tolerate being hated and to be able to say no is probably more significant than the loving. To accept hatred without retaliation, while maintaining concern and acceptance, is the key to parenting, assuming that essential basic physical needs are met. It is crucial to see the child or young person as they really are and to hold onto one's sense of one's own adulthood and one's responsibilities in order to maintain the generational divide.

O'Hagen[3] has described the key tasks of adults responsible for children's social and emotional development:

*Early months*: the baby's achievement of a balanced state (feeding, sleeping, waking and eliminating);
*0 – 12 months*: the development of a secure attachment with a carer;
*12 – 30 months*: the development of an independent sense of self;

*Figure 1*
**A view of the whole child**

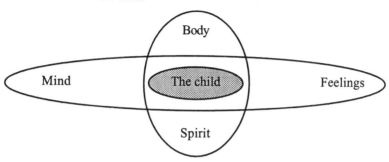

*Figure 2*
**Factors in understanding the whole child**

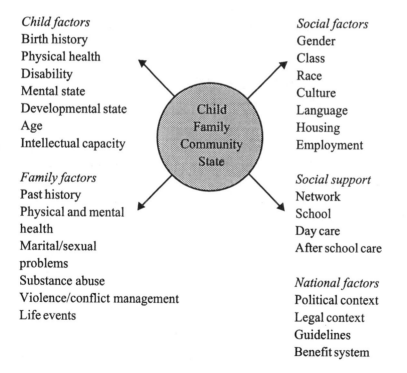

*Child factors*
Birth history
Physical health
Disability
Mental state
Developmental state
Age
Intellectual capacity

*Family factors*
Past history
Physical and mental
health
Marital/sexual
problems
Substance abuse
Violence/conflict management
Life events

*Social factors*
Gender
Class
Race
Culture
Language
Housing
Employment

*Social support*
Network
School
Day care
After school care

*National factors*
Political context
Legal context
Guidelines
Benefit system

*30 months – 7 years*: the establishment of peer relationships;
*7 – 12 years*: the integration of attachments, independence and peer relationships.

The effect of the process on the child, then, depends in large part on the parents' capacity to accomplish these tasks. To do so, they need to antici-pate difficulties, to empathise, to protect, to stimulate, to imagine what it is like to be a child, to make commitment, to show love and approval, and to let go and relinquish.

### Society's role

A fundamental conflict is the uncertainty in society about what con-stitutes abuse. The search for a universally agreed definition continues. Gabarino and Gallium[4] have produced one useful definition:

Child abuse is any act of omission or commission (by parent or guardian) that is judged by a mixture of community values and profes-sional expertise to be inappropriate or damaging.

In other words, professionals make value judgements on behalf of society and an assessment of abuse has to consider the pervasiveness, persistence and inflexibility of parental patterns.

This leads to the conclusion that protecting the child depends to a large extent on the skills, behaviour and attitudes of the adults around: parents, extended family, the community, the school, and primary health care. There must also be a continuum between good enough and unacceptable parenting, with a cut off point agreed by society. If this is the case, then the importance of preventive work and early intervention is highlighted, because if a smaller input early on can prevent the slide into bad parenting and harm to the child, it would appear to make sense to invest one's resources in this work. It does seem that in the wake of the publication, *Child Protection: Messages from research*,[5] that this has been recognised although the resource implications are not likely to be recognised and addressed.

At present, it seems that there is no policy or guidance to enforce or ensure preventive work. On the contrary, support services and early inter-vention are being run down. Entry on the child protection register is in many places the gateway to services, which means that services are only mobilised when there is harm or grave concern. Action to protect the child through the court requires evidence of damage to the child, that is, significant harm or likelihood of significant harm. We have seen in Chapter 2 that agreement about what constitutes significant harm and proving it has been shown to be problematic.

**Protection or therapy**
The therapeutic option for the child and the family only becomes available after serious concerns have arisen. But is the system set up to be therapeutic? Regrettably, it seems not.[6] Moreover, each change in law or in guidance and procedures that corrects some of the problems only throws up others. Before the Children Act 1989, the child frequently had no voice and was subject to repeated interviewing. Decision making was patchy and inconsistent and many cases went into drift. The Children Act is one of the most enlightened pieces of legislation affecting children anywhere. Judges and magistrates are much better trained and work to timetables to prevent delay; the child can have independent representation and/or be represented by a guardian; and the extended family and unmarried fathers can become parties.

But the negatives are emerging. For example, the *Memorandum of Good Practice*[7] endorsed the practice of one interview only and imposed time limits. This seems good, but in practice it means that children often do not find it possible to talk the first and only time they are interviewed. In addition, since the law has to be involved with any change of plan, directions hearings have become overwhelming in number, taking up a great deal of court time. Cases are not reserved; so continuity and knowledge of the case can be lost as different judges hear the case when it returns to court for each of the hearings.

The process for the child can be seen as having improved but it has become much more regulated by law and guidance. The question remains: how therapeutic is the process for the child? This depends on the qualities of the adults, but with the involvement of professionals, the risk of secondary abuse can increase considerably. For example, a child physically abused by his mother was removed and placed with his aunt, the mother's sister. In turn, the aunt could not manage him and he was placed

69

with his maternal grandmother. Social services were very concerned about this placement. Frequently directions and interim care order hearings followed as the two extended families and social services disagreed and fought each other. The relationship between father and son was lost sight of, as social workers wrote off the whole family in their desperation to protect the boy. With each court hearing the boy became more depressed and withdrawn.

Professionals need to be well trained and have a good grasp of the assessment tasks. These include taking a history (both a general and an abuse history), observing the child, collecting information from the GP and the school, interviewing parents, siblings, the family and the child, as appropriate. They must possess skills in communication and be aware of research findings. All of this cannot be done in isolation. It needs to be part of the local Working Together, interagency, interprofessional practice so that the different professionals contribute their skills, perspectives and understanding of children and families.

Whether the system is therapeutic or abusive will depend on the policies and procedures in place, the management and supervisory skills available, and the clarity professionals have of their role and task. Unfortunately, it may also depend on the professional's capacity to write good reports and present well in court, rather than on the clinical skills and capacity to make objective decisions. The latter comes about because the decision making frequently happens in court, with its adversarial approach. Witnesses are cross-examined, and their capacity to respond to questioning, rather than the best interests of the child, may influence the outcome. For example, child psychiatrists report how they often find themselves seeing attendance at court either as a part of a game or as being on trial themselves. When it is a game, they enter into the cross-examination as a point-scoring exercise, a battle of intellects between the lawyer and the psychiatrist. When they feel on trial, they act defensively.

Either situation can result in the child disappearing from view. What seems to matter is not the child's best interest, but the reputation of the psychiatrist. Other more therapeutic systems exist, such as the Scottish Children's Hearings or the Judge for Children in France. These systems focus on what is best for the child given the existing circumstances, rather than on why the situation has arisen.

Once decisions are made, however they are arrived at, questions arise about what exists by way of support and what possibility there is of working on the problems at this secondary stage. Regrettably, there is no more provision at this stage than there was for primary prevention. On the whole, children who have actually been harmed or are at serious risk of harm are better protected, but this often consumes all the resources allocated for child protection. Yet the needs of children at lesser risk are also great. They need good, well-supported placements with the nonabusing parent or substitute carer. They need individual and group therapy. They may need special education. The adults involved need help; the abuser needs therapy; the whole family needs input. The parents need help with parenting skills and probably with their relationship. Much or most of this is not available.

In my experience, as indicated earlier, a large number of sexually abused girls interviewed say that they want the abuse to stop, but they want to be in a united family even though going back might mean abuse again. What they have now is worse, they say. For example, two sisters who had been sexually abused by the consecutive cohabitees of their mother were placed in a foster family which had three of their own children. One of the sisters settled but the other became increasingly distressed. She was able to talk about how much she missed her mother. She felt that the foster mother was trying to take the mother's place, and she couldn't bear this. She knew that she might be abused again if she lived with her mother, but that is the place she wanted to be.

The care we are offering such children, most of whom have had no therapeutic post-protection work, seems to be sadly lacking. The process for them is painful and they are left feeling isolated and unhappy, wondering what has improved. The abuse has stopped, but so much else has been lost.

### References
1   Gillick v West Norfolk and Wisbech Health Authority and the DHSS (1985) 3 ALL ER 402.

2   Browne K D, Davenport C, and Palmer R, 'Opinions on the traumatising effects of child sexual abuse: evidence for consensus', *International Journal*

*of Child Abuse and Neglect*, 18:9, 725-738, 1994.

3   O'Hagen K, *Emotional and Psychological Abuse of Children*, Open University Press, 1994.

4   Gabarino J, and Gallium G, *Understanding Abusive Families*, Lexington Books, 1980.

5   Department of Health, *Child Protection: Messages from research*, HMSO, 1995.

6   King M, and Trowell J A, *Children's Welfare and the Law: The limits of legal intervention*, Sage Publications, 1992.

7   *Memorandum of Good Practice on video interviews of child witnesses*, Home Office and Department of Health, 1992.

# 7 Reassessing protectiveness

*Gerrilyn Smith*

*Gerrilyn Smith is a Clinical Psychologist, Family Therapist, Trainer and Consultant with expertise on issues of abuse in families.*

In this chapter, the author proposes a rethink about how best to protect children from abuse, particularly sexual abuse. She offers a reconceptualisation of Finkelhor's model and looks to the strengthening of the natural network as fundamental to greater success.

It is essential that we reconsider how best to protect our children. The media attention to professional protection services often portrays them as over-zealous, yet is quick to condemn them as a failure on other occasions. I think this reflects the deep ambivalence we have as a society not only about who should be responsible for protecting children but also how best to protect them.

## Phase 1: Children as their own protectors

In the mid 1980s the answer to child protection seemed to rest in prevention programmes in schools. The message was for children to *say no*. The realisation that this was not enough came quickly[1] and the programmes were modified to encourage children to *tell*. But fundamentally the message was still the same – it was the children's responsibility to protect themselves rather than an adult's responsibility both to refrain from abusing them in the first place and protect them from abuse in the second. A similar pattern can be observed in the recent campaign regarding bullying which concentrates on what to do if you are bullied but remains remarkably silent about not becoming a bully in the first place.

The more important message aimed at preventing children and young people from becoming coercive in the first place, whether that means bullying, being sexually aggressive, racist or sexist is still a long way off. Even David Finkelhor's Four Preconditions Model[2] implied that the

73

greatest burden of protection rested with factor four: the child's capacity to resist. Traditionally it was represented diagrammatically as follows:

*Figure 1*
**Four preconditions of sex abuse**

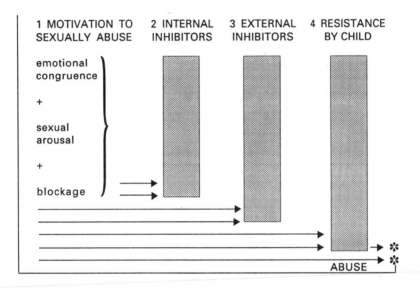

In trying to reconceptualise the approach to child protection work, I started by adapting the Four Preconditions model so that the burden of the task of prevention, protection and recovery should rest with the adults that surround children, the natural network (see *Figure 2*).

I also place 'X's to mark the boundary violations that occur whenever a factor does not effectively inhibit the progression from sexually abusive thought to sexually abusive action. In this way it becomes clearer where to aim some of our interventions in child protection services when we cannot access alleged offenders to help treat their problem.

While the model has been specifically developed for sexual abuse, I think that it can be usefully applied to other sorts of abuse. If we think about the idea of progression from thought to action, perhaps thinking about hitting a child is the first step towards doing it in reality. However, unlike sexual

## Figure 2
**Finkelhor's four preconditions, adapted by Gerrilyn Smith**

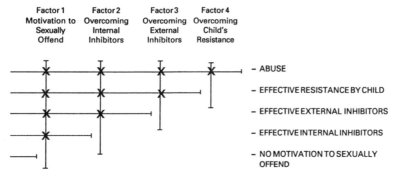

| Factor 1 | Factor 2 | Factor 3 | Factor 4 |
|---|---|---|---|
| Motivation to Sexually Offend | Overcoming Internal Inhibitors | Overcoming External Inhibitors | Overcoming Child's Resistance |

- ABUSE

- EFFECTIVE RESISTANCE BY CHILD

- EFFECTIVE EXTERNAL INHIBITORS

- EFFECTIVE INTERNAL INHIBITORS

- NO MOTIVATION TO SEXUALLY OFFEND

abuse, thoughts of physically chastising children are not considered reprehensible in our culture. To find adults sharing their feelings about wanting to smother, strangle, or murder their child is not uncommon. They are likely to get sympathetic responses from other adults because we all assume that we are speaking metaphorically and that we wouldn't really do what we are saying. Apart from this, talking about your feelings alleviates the need to do the things you think about, doesn't it?

I think this needs to be seriously reconsidered. We need to help each other as adults to find other things to *think* about doing when we are stressed by the demands of parenting.

### Phase 2: Focusing on conviction
Following the optimistic prevention programmes approach, child protection work became increasingly more preoccupied with the apprehension and conviction of offenders. This is epitomised by the *Memorandum of Good Practice on Video Recorded Interviews with Child Witnesses for Criminal Proceedings*[3] brought out in 1992. This guidance shapes the interviewing of children according to the requirements of criminal court cases by excluding any material that may be equivocal and putting maximum weight on spontaneous disclosures made by children to two unknown professionals in a 60 minute interview. These requirements have produced a tidal wave of anxiety in both primary caregivers and professionals alike regarding the use of leading questions. This sometimes spreads to even

talking about "it" at all. The prohibitions on speaking are so powerful that Crown Prosecution Services are being allowed to determine who can say what to the child pending the court case.

In one case I was involved with, the sisters had been told during their court case that they must not talk to each other *while the case was going on*. I use italics because this was not explicitly stated although it was clearly meant. Yet, six months *after* the case had folded because it would be unsafe to continue (meaning no convictions), the sisters still had not mentioned a word to each other about their experience of court or about the sexual abuse they almost certainly had experienced.

This preoccupation with offenders and the criminal justice system has led to what I call an "offender-organised" system of child protection. The services are now more focused on the "who done it" of sexual abuse rather than on what happened and how we can make sure it doesn't happen again

Resources have been concentrated on training investigators, especially with the introduction of the *Memorandum*. This focuses on Factors 1 and 2 of Finkelhor's model almost to the exclusion of all else. The new style of interviewing was supposed to radically transform child protection work. It has, but I think not in the best interests of children. Between October 1992 and June 1993, 14,912 video recorded interviews were conducted; 3,652 were sent to the Crown Prosecution Service and only 44 were admitted as evidence between January and June 1993.[4]

In the sample of children involved in *Messages from Children: Children's evaluations of the professional responses to child sexual abuse* study by NCH (Action for Children) and Guy's Hospital,[5] 110 of the 195 cases led to no prosecutions; 5 per cent received a police caution; 35 per cent were prosecuted. Of those prosecuted, 71 per cent were found guilty. Given that, in all of these cases, the balance of probability indicated that the children had indeed been sexually abused, this conviction rate of one in four is extremely low. This finding is replicated across the country. In Tower Hamlets, for example, from June 1991 to February 1992, out of 135 cases where sexual abuse was considered on balance of probability to have occurred, only two prosecutions were mounted.[6] The implications of these figures are depressing for two reasons. First and foremost for the child who may continue to experience sexual abuse simply because professional workers do not feel empowered to take statutory action in the absence of a clear verbal disclosure made during a video recorded interview. Second, to the professional system itself, which has expended so much professional time and expertise on the interviewing to little effect. The concentration of resources on investigation was meant to result in more prosecutions and, concomitantly, more convictions.

These figures also have to be viewed alongside the finding by Liz Kelly, Linda Reagan and Sheila Burton that, of those in their sample who had experienced sexual abuse, only 50 per cent told someone, and of those, only five per cent told a statutory agency.[7] Consequently it is essential that we empower, inform and educate children's natural networks to be more effective in preventing, protecting and facilitating the recovery from sexual abuse.

**Phase 3: Empowering natural networks**
This model proposes that we concentrate on helping what is termed "external inhibitors" to become more effective. This assigns the primary responsibility of preventing sexual abuse to the offenders, but it also gives the rest of the non-abusing adults a substantive role to play in child protection. Establishing a protected environment needs consideration. Our prevention programmes should be aimed first at the adults who surround children in their day-to-day lives: parents, extended family members, childminders, nursery workers, and teachers among others.

It is clear that when the only protector for a child is a statutory worker the risks for future abuse are extremely great. The amount of training and resources allocated to non-abusing parents is negligible.[8] Only fractionally better is the amount allocated for alternative family placements calculated at a paltry £35 per annum.[9] Yet the importance that the child's network plays in both preventing and facilitating the recovery from sexual abuse has been clearly documented in many research studies.[10] These studies indicate that a parent's belief in the child mitigates against the negative consequences of sexual abuse.

*Figure 3* tries to focus our minds on making child protection truly child centred.

In Circle A the child is surrounded by a community of adults where one cannot tell who might be a perpetrator and who a possible protector. In this configuration our efforts must be to empower both children and the adults

*Figure 3*

**The offender-organised system: keeping it child-centred**

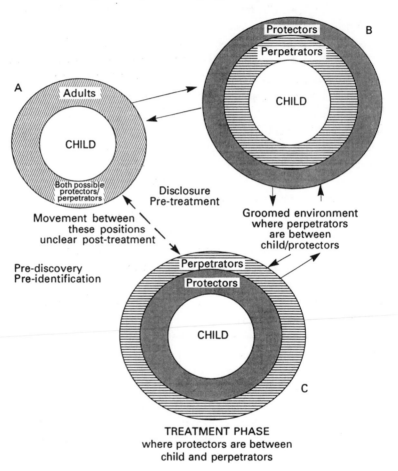

who surround them to understand what constitutes sexual abuse, how to recognise the signs or indicators that it may be happening and what to do if they think it is. This requires not only a sensitivity to observing inter-actions between children and adults, or indeed other juveniles as Jamie Bulger's case taught us, but also to be able to intervene assertively, effectively and appropriately. For example, there were adults who came into contact with Jamie Bulger as he was being led away to his death. Intuitively they perceived something wasn't right but they did not feel they could intervene for a whole variety of reasons. Expecting Jamie to say no, then run away and tell can be seen to be unbelievably naïve. Yet, had we targeted adults for the early prevention and protection messages so current in the eighties – 'trust your funny feelings', 'tell someone you trust and get help' – the adult community that surrounded Jamie Bulger might have been more effective at intervening and preventing his death. There were missed opportunities, opportunities to have done something that could have made a difference. We can see from that profoundly disturbing experience that we, as a community of adults, are reluctant to take responsibility for protecting other people's children. Hence protectiveness has become increasingly professionalised and more removed from the natural networks that surround children where it would be most effective.

In Circle B the perpetrators and possible protectors become more differentiated. Perpetrators will strive to place themselves closest to the child with possible protectors at a greater distance. This is termed the "groomed environment". In this situation, the perpetrator will attempt to control information in and out of the family. This is important to consider, especially in light of the welcome move to include parents in case conferences. How can we ensure that the conference itself doesn't become preoccupied by an offender-organised agenda? Child protection needs to remain central. The signs and indicators need to be spelt out and methods of reducing any perceived risks need to be clearly identified. Some attempt has to be made to hear all points of view. Systems that function effectively, whether families or case conferences, should be able to provide a context for all points of view to be aired, bearing in mind that the rights of the child should supersede those of the adults. In this interim stage of the statutory child protection process, the need for clearly identified protectors is paramount. How can families demonstrate that they can protect their children? How can statutory agencies help them with that task?

Circle C indicates the context for recovery. Here the potential protectors are closest to the child with potential perpetrators at a greater distance. Initially this may be a geographical distance but over time it must move to include a psychological distance. This means challenging the construction of the world that is being reinforced by the perpetrator.

Not only must issues regarding responsibility and collusion be included, but also, and fundamentally, belief that abuse has taken place. In the absence of this belief, recovery is not possible. This issue then becomes the cornerstone of assessing a non-abusing parent's capacity to protect.[11] Helping non-abusing parents assess the evidence and understand the risks involved in some actions, such as living with a Schedule 1 offender, should form a significant part of our professional interventions.

Professional protectors, foster carers and residential workers need to be functioning at the highest level of protectiveness. As a consequence, they should be targeted for specific training to help increase their skills. This includes not only the primary prevention material messages, such as what sexual abuse is, how to recognise it, and what to do if you think it has happened, but also the more complex issues of helping children begin the recovery process living away from their families of origin.

The importance of protection through the child's natural network is especially relevant in black and other minority ethnic communities. The pressure to keep quiet can be even greater for them. However, black survivors have begun to speak out publicly about their experiences, risking criticism from their own communities for placing private matters into the white public domain.[12] It is vital that survivors in any minority group maintain their place within the community and receive support and help from members of their community. A healing message from me as a white woman may be comforting to a black child, but the same message from another black person will reverberate and resonate much more for that child.

### Conclusion

Instilling knowledge and skills into the community about the reality of sexual abuse and how to help reduce the risks must be an essential part of an overall child protection strategy. Prevention of child sexual abuse must be the long-term aim of that strategy. To achieve such an idealistic goal, one which I think I will not see in my lifetime, we must operate and provide services that cover all of the four factors identified in David Finkelhor's model. The importance of involving the community is both a short-term necessity and a long-term goal. Already a substantial proportion of child protection is dealt with by the community.[13] We need more information on how effective it is. We need information on sexual abuse and sexual knowledge available not only to children through education programmes in schools but also to their parents. This will enable any protection strategies to grow and develop with the child. We need to be able to communicate about difficult and uncomfortable topics, supported and nurtured through school programmes. We need better communication between adults in the community to foster the view that the safety and protection of children is truly a shared responsibility.

## References

1 Mills J C, 'Putting Ideas into their Heads: Advising the Young', *Feminist Review* No 28, 1988.

2 Finkelhor D, 'Four Preconditions: A model', in *Child Sexual Abuse: New theory and research*, Free Press, Collier Macmillan, 1984.

3 Department of Health and Home Office, *The Memorandum of Good Practice on Video Recorded Interviews with Child Witnesses for Criminal Proceedings*, HMSO, 1992.

4 Daily Telegraph, 29 November 1994.

5 Prior V, Lynch M, and Glaser D, *Messages from Children: Children's evaluations of the professional response to child sexual abuse*, Interim Report, NCH Action for Children, 1994.

6 Austin A, *Analysis of CSA Referrals from Police Records*, Unpublished paper for Tower Hamlets ACPC, 1992.

7 Kelly L, Regan L, and Burton S, *An Exploratory Study of the Prevalence of Sexual Abuse in a Sample of 16 – 21 Year Olds*,' Polytechnic of North London: Child Abuse Studies Unit, 1991.

8 Hooper C, *Mothers Surviving Child Sexual Abuse*, Routledge, 1992.

9 Borthwick S, personal communication.

10 Wyatt G, and Mickey M, 'The Support of Parents and Others as it Mediates the Effects of Child Sexual Abuse', in Wyatt G, and Powell G (eds), *Lasting Effects of Child Sexual Abuse*, Sage, 1988.

11   Smith G, 'Parent, Partner and Protector: Conflicting role demands for mothers of sexually abused children', in Morrison T, Erooga M, and Beckett R, *Sexual Offending Against Children: Assessment and treatment of male abusers*, Routledge, 1994.

12   Wilson M, *Crossing the Boundary: Black women survive incest*, Virago, 1993.

13   See 7 above.

# 8 Supporting the carers to ensure safe caring

*Ena Fry*

*Since 1990 Ena Fry has been Development Worker attached to NFCA's Young People's Project prior to which she worked in a range of residential and fieldwork settings mainly as a practitioner.*

**Foster care is widely recognised as crucial to providing substitute care for children and young people who need it. Yet foster carers and their families are not always given the support they need to ensure safe caring. The author here sets out a framework of support that should satisfy the needs of both carers and the cared for, paying particular attention to guarding against abuse by a foster family and dealing with families where abuse of foster children has been alleged.**

## Introduction
*Child protection and foster care*
Foster care is now the first option chosen by the majority of agencies for children and young people requiring safe substitute care. The decision that any child subject to child protection proceedings should not remain with his or her family, temporarily or in the longer term, will therefore require the agency to consider the appropriateness of foster care, the role of the foster family, and the support systems required to carry out the individual child care plan.

The National Foster Care Association (NFCA) is a membership organisation reflecting the experiences and views of foster carers, social work staff and other professionals as well as users (young people and their families). This constituency has informed our understanding of how fostering affects foster families and what preparation and continuing support is needed to provide safe care.

Child protection can affect foster families in two main ways:

1 In all instances, foster carers are part of the professional team offering

skilled help/care to the child and his or her family.

2  In some instances, a carer or a member of their family may be subject to a child protection investigation as a result of an allegation that they have abused a child in their household or previously in their care.

The emphasis on partnership within the Children Act 1989 makes the establishment of a good working relationship between a foster family and an agency the central element in ensuring quality care for every child. Partnership and good practice require agencies to perceive and treat foster carers not as clients but as a key resource.

Foster care is well suited to meet the therapeutic aspects of child protection work. It provides care within a family setting and within the community. The diversity of foster families accommodates linguistic, cultural and religious differences. The ultimate aim for everyone is to help a child or young person come to terms with past experiences by working through confused, powerful feelings in order to make some sense of their own lives, to strengthen their self-esteem and to develop their own protective strategies. Strong feelings are often acted out in ways that are demanding for carers, placing them at risk from false allegations or even secondary abuse of the child. It is the responsibility of every agency to recognise this and to emphasise prevention in training programmes for carers. This approach will strengthen the working partnership with foster families and contribute to the therapeutic environment for the child.

Most foster families work closely and effectively with colleagues as part of a professional team. The team draws on the foster family's specialist skills, expertise and training, which will include:

- knowledge of child development, including the effects of abuse;
- ability to understand and work with a wide range of behavioural problems;
- in-depth experience of working with a range of children and their families;
- sensitivity to, and ability to communicate with, parents who may be very distressed and angry;
- experience in helping children to return to their birth families or join an adoptive family;
- assessment skills;

- report writing and other relevant skills including participation in planning meetings and court work.

The reality of foster care is that many foster children will always wish that they could live with their birth families at home. This feeling persists even in children who have been abused. Through training and open dialogue with their agency, foster families can learn to recognise and deal with the children's pain rather than seeing it as overt rejection of their care.

*Current child protection issues*
Other chapters in this book have highlighted recent research studies demonstrating that the focus of child protection work has been on investigation rather than therapy. Redressing this imbalance and interpreting therapy as including intervention has implications for foster care.

Celia Atherton, co-Director of the Family Rights Group, in a recent meeting referred to the views expressed by many professionals that child protection work is 'becoming increasingly divorced from mainstream work with families. . . it is essential to work with families before their problems become acute. That means creating an effective partnership within the community, raising awareness of child protection issues.' Likewise, effective foster care is dependent on a good working partnership between foster families, agencies and the child's family.

Foster families need to be empowered to help children through procedures that may be as traumatic as the original abuse. Indeed, adults in the process often feel powerless, with long periods of apparent inactivity interspersed with crisis or action points such as case conferences or court appearances. The foster family is a consistent part of the child's life throughout this period, so it is crucial that their role be understood, valued and supported. However, the status of foster carers is a complex one and not as easily understood as the parent/child one. This is highlighted particularly when an allegation of abuse is made.

*Position of foster carers*
Fostering is a unique experience. Carers are subject to a detailed assessment process which explores in-depth attitudes about their family, their life experiences, their sexuality and sexual relationships. Whether the re-

cruitment approach has been to depict fostering as helping a needy child or as a professional task, carers will be challenged by agency staff to reveal their innermost feelings.

On being accepted by an agency, carers feel a strong sense of responsibility and expect to be valued as colleagues by the agency and others. Training should further reinforce their sense of worth and their role in a working partnership where their views ought to be sought and respected. However, while Foster Care Regulations require agencies to spell out the terms and conditions of their foster care service, agencies are not required to clarify the status of carers. So expectations and reality may differ.

*Children are not dangerous – situations can be*
In trusting foster families with the day-to-day care of vulnerable, damaged children and young people who may have been subject to multiple abuse, agencies have a responsibility to:

- recognise and address the heightened vulnerability of foster families;
- provide appropriate training for the possibility that a member of the foster family may be the first recipient of a child's disclosure;
- ensure that prospective and approved foster families understand why and how they must provide "safe caring" to minimise the risk of further abuse and at the same time protect all members of the family.

For their part, the carers' responsibility is to ensure that the foster home is a safe place for everyone living there, especially foster children joining the family.

**The foster carer's role within the child protection team**
*Assessment*
Prior to accepting foster carers, procedures can be used to strengthen the partnership. From the assessment stage onwards, support for the carers needs to be reassessed regularly at the annual review required by the Foster Care Regulations, at case conferences, at placement meetings, and during individual work between the foster family and social workers. As all members of the foster family are involved in the care of abused children, foster families must understand that:

- the values and routines that children bring from their birth families are likely to be very different from those in a non-abusive foster home;

- serious misunderstandings can arise from the impact of these differences on life in the foster home;
- the psychological effects of caring for children who have been abused may well change over time as the foster family itself changes through internal and external circumstances.

The assessment stage is the foundation of the partnership. The emphasis needs to be joint exploration of the foster family's attitudes and values, particularly in relation to:

- loss/change;
- sex, sexuality and sex education;
- gender differences;
- differing life styles and cultures;
- religion;
- disability;
- abuse;
- problem-solving/managing behaviour;
- communication within the family;
- links with the community.

Exploring these areas in depth gives the family an opportunity to consider how they function as a family; what their values and attitudes are and how open to change they are. This process helps them to assess the impact fostering will have on their family. At this stage, careful consideration should be given to the concept of "open" or "closed" families. An open family is flexible and can handle change; a closed one or one that is more rigid, resisting and rejecting change. Careful consideration should also be given to issues of religion, culture and gender. Agency workers undertaking this assessment must themselves be able to discuss these issues in an open, non-judgemental way.

*Preparing for the placement of an abused child*
All members of the family will be involved using both individual and group work and training focused on:

- caring for a child who has been abused;

- the legal framework within which child protection work is undertaken including the role of other professionals, constraints, child protection procedures, outcomes and complaints procedures;
- strategies for safe caring within the foster home covering daily activities, such as bed and bathtime routines, dress, privacy, travelling in the car, and so on;
- confidentiality and record keeping by the foster family and the agency.

### In placement

The emphasis in placement will be on reviewing the range of support needed with the foster family. This will include:

- *Information*

  Information is empowering; it can help the child both to feel safe and be safe and it can help the carer both to feel safe and act safely. Carers need to know everything there is to know about the child unless there are specific reasons against this, for example, when a birth parent has requested this but a distinction should always be made between *fact* and *opinion*.

  The more information a foster family can have, preferably in advance of the placement, the easier it is to provide therapeutic care for a child who has been abused. Also, information is the basis on which carers can decide whether or not a child is right for them. Information gathering is a continuing element in the placement. It must be based on a shared approach, so strengthening the working partnership.

Information falls broadly into three main categories:
1. Information about the child and the birth family. This helps the foster family provide appropriate and immediate continuing care and ensures its availability for children in the future if they do not return to their birth families.
2. Information about any abuse the child has experienced: by whom; its nature; the circumstances in which it took place; the action taken; the child's feelings and reactions.
3. Information a child would find helpful about the foster family.

- *Clarifying tasks*

  A placement agreement meeting is a cornerstone of good practice. It identifies the roles and responsibilities each party has in the individual child care plan. Regular reviews and periodic communication meetings ensure that everyone's voice is heard, including the child's, and that information is shared and acted on in the child's interest.

- *Respite*
  Respite should be built in at the beginning of the placement and regularly reviewed so that carers are not overstretched. Careful consideration has to be given to babysitters: who they are, their suitability, preparation and confidentiality.

- *Therapy*
  Carers should be informed of what therapy is available within reach of the foster home, for whom and when. There should be contingency plans if therapy is delayed and regular communication between the therapist and the carers should be arranged. If therapy is either not available or not considered necessary, alternative sources of support should be identified for the carers in dealing with the child's reactions to abuse.

- *Endings*
  All members of the foster family should have an opportunity to feed back their views and experiences and contribute to either a smooth return home or a move to another family.

It also includes strategies for letting go; that is the future role of the family who have played a key part at a significant time in a child's life.

### Allegations of abuse within the foster home
*Dealing with the feelings involved*
'Until recently, concerns about children in foster care have centred on the child's past experience of abuse rather than any current protection. The response to reports of sexual abuse by carers has been one of concern, confusion and defensiveness.'[1]

This quote focuses on the second numbered point made at the beginning of this chapter, that is, an allegation of abuse against a member of a foster family. It is first necessary at an early stage to identify strategies to reduce the risk of false allegations, and then to address sensitively the needs of the minority of foster families who find themselves subject to formal investigatory procedures as the result of an allegation.

When an allegation is made, agency staff often feel acutely uncomfortable as the "colleague" is now a "client". It is the agency's responsibility to ensure that this shift is managed in a humane and fair way, as should happen for any family. It must be recognised that the situation would not have arisen in the first place had the family not come forward and been accepted to foster.

The agency's task is to provide a framework within which:

• foster families are enabled, through training and careful preparation for each placement, to play their part confidently, safely and appropriately in caring for the child and to contribute fully within the professional team;

• the risk of false allegations is addressed during assessment, training and preparation and therefore substantially reduced;

• the needs of foster families are sensitively considered by the agency if an allegation leads to a formal investigation.

*Reducing risk*

It has to be acknowledged that a small number of people will apply to foster because they see it as an opportunity to abuse children. No matter how stringent the assessment process, some people will "groom" workers and subsequently be approved as carers. Through increased vigilance and knowledge, this inevitability can be reduced, but the main focus must be on helping agencies reduce the greater risk of stress-related abuse by a carer or of false allegations by a child.

The way forward must include a reassessment of existing knowledge in terms of:

• current developments in child protection work as to what approaches contribute to or hinder the effectiveness of foster care as a key resource in meeting the needs of abused children and their families;

• the impact of allegations, false or substantiated, on foster families;

• the similarities and differences between foster families and others subject to allegations.

- the support systems that strengthen the partnership between foster carers, agencies and the child's birth family, in particular, the need for and practice of "safe caring" which takes into account cultural, racial and gender differences.

Through bitter experience, lessons are being learnt of how the past can impinge on the present. In providing "therapeutic" care to children who have been abused, foster carers and their families expose themselves to intense feelings and behaviour that, unless properly understood, place them at risk. Research studies have highlighted the increased likelihood of a member of a foster family having an allegation or complaint made against them. One in six foster carers in a Birmingham University study,[2] for example, had a complaint made against them at some time in their fostering career. Research by Wisconsin University[3] in the USA concluded that foster families are twice as likely to have an allegation made against them as other members of the general public.

The impact of any allegation on a foster family is profound. It affects them in a myriad of ways, among others, the abrupt removal of foster children and sometimes their own; the withdrawal of a fostering worker at a crisis time; the investigatory process; and the loss of status, a loss which may lead to feelings akin to those of bereavement. It is often the more experienced foster carers who are asked to care for the most troubled children so that when allegations are made against them, their loss of standing in the local community can be very great.

It is common practice that contact between an agency and foster families is usually with the female carer. At one level, that may be more practicable but it should not be the basis for a working partnership. Given the considerable evidence that the majority of sexual abusers are heterosexual men, the assessment stage is crucial in:

- acknowledging the higher risks inherent in a heterosexual household;
- setting a framework in assessment and preparation to explore the role of male members of the family and their involvement in the direct care of children;
- setting the pattern for including male family members in regular statutory reviews of the foster family undertaken by the agency;

- ensuring that male members of a household understand their vulnerability under stress, and leading to the possibility of abuse.

The work of the NFCA's mediation service endorses the need for this approach. This confidential service has been developed in response to the increasingly complex demands placed on foster families. The objects of the service are:

- to offer independent advice and support to foster carers where they need help from outside the agency, for example, complaints by carers about agency decisions or allegations of abuse against a member of the foster family;
- to mediate between the foster family and the agency when invited to do so;
- to contribute to agency policies, procedures and training programmes which promote "safe caring" and help to keep allegations and complaints to a minimum.

There are NFCA advice and mediation workers in various parts of the country and the service is expanding in response to local authority demand as it is seen as a valuable and necessary source of support.

Of 16 allegations of sexual abuse referred to one NFCA worker in 1992/93, 12 were against male carers and three against foster carers' sons. This highlights not only the need for male carers to participate fully in plans and training at all stages, but also for agencies to pay attention to the preparation of foster carers' own children. In particular, further work needs to be done on how to help carers and their children to examine sensitively relationships between young people who may be close in age (but not in maturity), background and life experiences.

Time spent on exploring current foster family practices and developing safe ones at the assessment stage can avoid crises later.

*Supporting the accused*

If an allegation is made against a member of the foster family, then good practice indicates that the carer has specific rights. They are:

- The right to be informed of the agency's anxiety and concern about the foster family and the quality of its care.

- The right to be told in writing the substance of the complaint.
- The right to place on record their perception of events when they believe that the agency either has been misinformed or has received inaccurate information.
- The right to be heard by people with relevant experience who are not directly involved in the complaint.
- The right to a proper investigation by competent and experienced people who are independent of the child and foster carer.
- The right to support acceptable to the carer while the investigation proceeds and after it has reported its findings. This support can come from link workers, voluntary self-help groups or independent counsellors/social workers.
- The right to receive in writing details of decisions made and action taken.
- The right to appeal.
- The right to arrange legal representation.

## Conclusion

Foster care has a crucial part to play in redressing the imbalance providing as it does opportunities for children and their families to receive consistent, skilled help on a daily basis. It requires social work agencies and other professionals to understand that, when provided with thorough training and support, foster families become an integral part of the professional team and make a unique and valuable contribution. This requires a significant shift in attitude in some agencies and in other professional disciplines involving child protection, so that foster carers are treated as colleagues with more emphasis on joint training. It also requires a commitment to safe caring practices within the foster home which also recognises the heightened vulnerability of foster families to false allegations and secondary abuse.

In this chapter I have set out the framework of support that should ensure safe caring in a foster home. In doing so, I have to conclude that, if such support were available to the children and their families of origin at an earlier stage, prevention rather than prosecution would be the outcome in many instances. This is a belief which many experienced foster carers hold themselves.

## References

1   Boushel M, 'Keeping Safe: Strengthening the protective environment of chldren in foster care', *Adoption & Fostering*, 18:1, BAAF, 1994.

2   Nixon S and Hicks C, *Allegations of Child Abuse: Foster carers as victims*, University of Birmingham, 1989.

3   Carbino R (ed), *Consequences of Child Abuse: Allegations for Foster families*, Madison Health and Human Issues, University of Wisconsin, 1991, USA.

## Further reading

Bolton F, Morris L, MacCullen A, *Males at Risk*, Sage Publications, 1989.

Fahlberg V, *A Child's Journey through Placement*, UK edition, BAAF, 1994.

McFadden E, *Preventing Abuse in Foster Care*, Ypsilanti, Michigan, National Foster Care Education Project, Eastern Michigan University, 1984, USA.

Moorat D, 'Allegations against carers', *Foster Care* no.68, December 1991.

Nixon S, and Hicks C, *Unsubstantiated Accusations of Abuse: A survey of foster carers experiences*, 1989.

## NFCA (National Foster Care Association) publications/materials:

*Choosing to Foster – the challenge to care*, 1994. Training pack with particular reference to Session 3 'Working Together', Session 5 'Fostering and your Family', Session 8 'Sex and Sexuality'.

*Safe Caring*, 1994. A practical guide to understanding why and how to make a foster home a safe place for all its members.

Signpost series: *Fostering a Child who has been Sexually Abused*, 1995.

Signpost series: *Child Abuse: Accusations against foster carers*, 1995.

Making it work series: *Managing Abuse Allegations*: Specific guidance for agencies on managing allegations made against foster families.

Making it work series: *Assessment*: Measuring competence, home visits, giving full information and involving applicants in the process.

# 9 Prevention and Éducation in work with children and families

*Rachael Hetherington*

*Rachael Hetherington is a Lecturer in Social Work at Brunel University College.*

Social work with children and families in the United Kingdom has been struggling for some time to maintain itself in the face of continuing pressures for preventive work to be subsumed by child protection. This chapter draws on research into child protection in England and France in looking at the possibility that social work in other European countries can offer new perspectives on problems in this country.

## A French case study

Michelle, a French social worker, is describing one of her cases to her English colleague, Viv.

### Family history

The Laville family has been known to the DASS (Social Services Department of the local authority) for several years, since their 14-year-old was five. The initial referral came from the infant school: teachers expressed general anxieties over the fluctuating level of care, their concern remaining constant. The Laville children were dirty, they missed school and occasionally had unexplained bruises. The family had help in various forms, from a family aide, from the health visitor, from an auxiliary health visitor, with budgeting and with group activities for the children, which they always accepted. Things improved, then always slipped back to where they had been before. Faced with this repeated cycle, the DASS decided that a more comprehensive approach was needed, and referred the family to *Aide Sociale à l'Enfance* (ASE), the specialist children's service within the social services department. The manager of this service (called the *Inspec-*

*teur*) met with the parents and offered them the alternatives of referral to the Judge for Children or a voluntary supervision order, to work with a specialist social worker from a voluntary agency on their family problems. The parents were not enthusiastic about the supervision order but, faced with the alternative, they agreed.

It was on this basis of grudging acceptance by the parents that Michelle had started work with the family. It was not a promising situation, but it was a familiar one to both Michelle and Viv.

The family consisted of M and Mme Laville and their three children, Genevieve, aged 14 (stepdaughter to M Laville), Bernard, aged 10 and Cecile, aged six. Both the parents had had difficult childhood experiences, and M Laville was now an alcoholic. The children were physically neglected, the house was dirty, and communication within the family was poor. The children were all enuretic and were ostracised at school as a result. There were also more disquieting aspects to the family situation: both the girls had intermittent stomach pains, for which the parents did not seek medical help, and Bernard's provocative behaviour led to trouble at school.

'Supervision order' is an approximate translation for the French order for *Action Éducative en Milieu Ouvert* (AEMO). The aim is intervention which is educational in the broadest sense. The child remains at home. The work is with the whole family, and an AEMO can be either *administratif*, that is, voluntary, as with the Laville family, or *judiciare*, that is, imposed by the Judge for Children. The difference in the name, supervision as opposed to *Action Éducative*, is important. It reflects a difference in orientation between France and England that pervades work with children and families: there is more emphasis in France on preventive work and a greater expectation that families will be able to change.

**The process of the work**
How did the AEMO for the Laville family work in practice? The initial order was for three months and, in the setting up of the order, Michelle agreed a plan of work with the family. She saw it as paramount to establish a trusting

relationship with them. Her aim was to work with the family as a whole and with individuals within a framework of systemic theory. She worked with the parents about establishing boundaries, for instance, she tried to discourage having Cecile sleep in her parents' bedroom. She worked with them all about difficulties in communication. She made home visits, liaised with the children's schools and with the health services of the DASS, still involved with Cecile. In July she arranged for Genevieve to go on a mini camp and went on it herself. She worked on hygiene with the children, helping them herself to clean their bedrooms. The family agreed to a six month extension of the order.

Michelle was supported in this work by her agency. The team consisted of eight social workers, a psychologist, a sessional child psychiatrist and a team leader. This team is part of a range of services provided to the local authority by a nationally established voluntary organisation. This particular team was contracted by the local authority to take a certain number of AEMO orders per year, mainly *judiciare*, but also *administratif*. In addition to the team, Michelle could also consult the team psychologist, a systemic family therapist. Her anxiety about the family required this support. She thought it possible that the children were being sexually abused, but could only conjecture.

In view of the fact that the parents were co-operating, she did not think it appropriate to refer them to the children's judge. If the family had been plainly unco-operative, that would have given her grounds for a referral. She did not, in a sense recognisable in English law, have to *prove* that the children were suffering significant harm. It would have been sufficient that the parents were not working with her positively. Her problem was that M and Mme Laville were working with her, but without much enthusiasm. Should she refer to the judge and get additional authority behind her, but lose the family's trust? Or should she continue to work on building trust to help the family to change?

Viv was clear that it would have been difficult for her to work without some involvement of the child protection system; she would at least have had to call a strategy meeting. This became more apparent as the case progressed.

Michelle continued to work according to her original plan. Genevieve and Bernard became involved in activities run by the agency. Genevieve's behaviour with boys seemed likely to lead her into trouble, and Bernard showed the provocative behaviour of which the school complained. There were some improvements in general hygiene, but Michelle's concern continued about the behaviour of Genevieve and Bernard, and about the possibility of sexual abuse. She raised this with Mme Laville and Genevieve, but both denied it.

Another order for six months was agreed with the family, and work continued in much the same way. Genevieve's school counsellor was concerned about her poor attendance and participation. A residential training school was suggested for Genevieve where she could get a catering qualification. This training school, run by a voluntary organisation, provides a resource for children and young people in need. There is some competition for admission.

A few months later, M Laville asked to see Michelle alone, and told her that he had been making improper sexual approaches to Genevieve and Bernard. He said that he was ashamed of this, but would not be more explicit. It happened when he was drunk and had been going on since they were about six. Michelle got his agreement to talk to Genevieve, but Genevieve continued to deny it. And there, at least for the moment, the matter rested. When the research project ended, negotiations were continuing for Genevieve to attend the training school with the financial support of the ASE and a parental contribution. No further progress had been made on the question of sexual abuse.

### The research project

Before considering the implications of this account, it is necessary to describe the research project[1] that is the source of the case material. The research aimed to compare systems and child protection practice in England and France. Ten English social workers were paired with ten French social workers. Over a nine-month period, they met five times, learning about each other's systems and following the progress of a representative case. The knowledge and understanding that they gained was relayed to both French and English research teams, who met regularly to collate information. An account of the outcomes of this research has been published.[2] It looks at the differences between the systems and a range of implications for practice. Here I examine in detail the way in which the French system seems to encourage an approach which is relatively optimistic about change, and which offers opportunities for preventive work which seem hard to achieve in England. First, here are some views from the participants.

Michelle and her English colleague, Viv, made interesting comments on their perceptions of each other's practice. Michelle said, 'Viv seemed very interested in procedures, she wanted to know what happens if a child discloses abuse.' Michelle explained that there was no set procedure, and what happens is decided according to circumstances. She felt that more weight was given to concrete factors in England. It was the sum of separate risk factors that influenced the decision making, rather than the totality of the situation. Viv felt that there was more focus on the family than on the child in France. Some aspects of the system made her wonder whether the child's rights were sufficiently protected. She said, 'Sometimes it is helpful to refer cases to a judge early; so often our court hearing comes too late because we have to have the evidence. This may cause more hostility than if a case had been referred at an earlier stage.'

**Implications of the Laville family case**

Michelle had two main concerns: on the one hand, she struggled to maintain a holistic approach to the family's problems, seeing the actions of the different members as symptoms of the family's problem. In order to work at this level, she had to establish herself as someone they could trust and with whom they could communicate. On the other hand, she had to be aware of concrete realities. Work included practical work around schooling and hygiene, as well as talking. Michelle commented that it was difficult to hold on to both these approaches when the family produced different problems at each visit. She had a lot of anxieties about this family, but her work was centred on helping them to change their behaviour and their patterns of communication.

She did not consider investigation a priority, even though she suspected sexual abuse: 'It was necessary to build an alliance with the family members so that they would co-operate sufficiently to engage in the work, and therefore one couldn't go too quickly into an investigation.' Her efforts to establish trust were effective in that they enabled M Laville to talk to her about his abusive actions. This acknowledgement, clearly made with difficulty, did not, however, solve the problem; Genevieve still denied having been abused.

At the point where information on this case ends, the situation is still precarious. On the plus side, the family acknowledges that they have problems, and some change is taking place. Michelle is still working with all family members and co-ordinates a support network.

Much about the way that Michelle worked with this family is familiar to British social workers, both in her aspirations and methods. Yet Viv thought that the case could not have had the same history in England. Why does it seem likely that this family's experience would have been so different in the English system?

**Key differences between the English and French systems**
Only the key differences between the systems can be described here. For more details, see Hetherington[3] and Cooper.[4] The ways in which structure and culture affect the function of a system are complex. Below, I examine ways in which they underlie the social work approach in the Laville case. The key structural differences between the French and English systems seem to facilitate the more process orientated and therapeutic French approach.

*Resources*
A high level of additional resources was invested in the Laville family both before and during Michelle's involvement. By the end of the research period, Michelle had been working intensively with the family for over a year and expected to continue. There did not seem to be any problem about maintaining this level of resourcing, nor was there any implication that it was unusual. This level of input to the family provided thorough monitoring of the children's state, but the main aim was to maintain and support the family.

*Entering the judicial system*
This case did not enter the judicial system, and it is interesting to explore why not in as much as other cases in the research made it plain that in France it is much easier to do so. Getting referred to the children's judge is not an index only of overt danger in the family situation, but indicates a

combination of danger with the extent of effective parental co-operation. In another project case, a family similar to the Lavilles was on a judicial AEMO, the difference being that the parents were much less ready to work with the social worker. Michelle described her position on potentially abusive physical punishment: 'One can accept that the parents are still hitting their children, if they acknowledge their difficulties and there seems to be a real capacity for change.'

Cases therefore develop along a different axis. If a child is seen to be suffering, there are grounds for intervention with the family. The first task is to build a relationship of trust enabling the family to work towards change. If this is successful, risks can be taken on the basis that the outcome in the long term will be better. If trust cannot be established, or the parents are actively unco-operative, then the case has to be referred to the children's judge. This judge brings in the authority of the office backed by the power to make a range of orders, including placement away from home. The referring social worker does not have to provide proof of harm; the judge, as the investigator, is responsible.

The judge, however, may not need proof in English terms. Ely and Stanley[5] describe a meeting between a family and a Children's Judge where a teenage girl had referred herself because she was afraid her father would hit her. Discussing the case afterwards, the authors asked whether there were any bruises. The judge replied: 'Whether it is true or false or not is not important. No, there were no bruises. What is certainly important is that we must get father and daughter back in communication with each other. There is something keeping them apart. What is important is not the blow but the relationship.'[6]

*The duty to investigate*

French social workers are not expected to investigate child protection cases on the basis that their findings will be used by the legal process. Michelle said that investigation had to take second place to establishing trust, using the word generally and not describing anything like a child abuse investigation. The French social workers were amazed by the importance of investigative work in England. The 'duty to investigate' that follows from Section 47 of the Children Act 1989 has had a powerful effect on social work practice in England, an unintended consequence of the legislation. The duty to investigate under the Children and Young Persons Act 1969 was broadened in the Children Act 1989.[7] It does not seem to have been a particularly controversial development, and Parton[8] does not mention it in discussing the parts of the legislation that were of 'political dispute and professional concern'.

On the other hand, the likelihood that the reduction of resources for social work in general would affect the implementation of the Act was foreseen. Parton points out that 'the Labour group (in parliament) in particular stressed that many of the good intentions of the Bill would be lost and a range of unintended consequences come about if the resources made available were inadequate.'[9] In fact, the process of reallocation of resources from child care to child protection was already well underway before the Children Act. Writing about changes that took place during the 1980s, Parton argues that 'the policies and professional practices previously designated as child care ... have not just been redesignated, but have been reconstructed around the axis of child protection.'[10]

The combination of a wider duty to investigate and the changes in priority described by Parton had several consequences for practice. If child protection is seen as the central duty of the social work service for children and families, then management is encouraged to investigate readily but the starting point will not be one that makes it easy to establish a working relationship. Enquiries then become a major time and resource consuming aspect of the work. Expertise is developed, several aspects of which impressed the French social workers.

One consequence, however, is that there is then less time to spend with families who are perhaps asking for help but, partly because they are taking this initiative, are not seen as needing investigation. Indeed there is less time to spend with families all round. A large number of investigations never lead to child protection conferences, let alone to court; but they take their toll on the families concerned.[11] Social services may be completely genuine in regarding the case as closed, but the families know there is a file with their name on it. This cannot help public confidence in social workers. The high profile of child protection investigation leads to an expense of time, expertise and emotional energy on this one aspect of work with families, and to a crisis orientated approach to work.

*Concepts of "the family"*

When we started our research, the English social workers at first saw the French families as having less power and fewer rights than English families. This position gradually changed, and we concluded that French families have different, not lesser, power and rights. French families appear to be less well protected from intervention, and their rights to know what is being planned and what is being said about them are less well established. However, the English research participants came to believe that the rights of the French families to be included in decision making, to be consulted and to be properly heard in the legal context, might be greater and more real. The framework of action for French parents is clear: they have more chance of knowing what is expected of them. In the first place, under the Civil Code they have a duty to protect, look after and educate their child ('educate' covers upbringing in a wider sense as well as schooling).[12] This is the bottom line, and is used by the children's judge as a reference point in talking with families. The family, both parents and children, can ask for an audience with the judge. It is therefore possible, as in the case quoted from Ely and Stanley,[13] for a child or a parent to take their family problems directly to the judge without the intervention of the social services.

The judge can make various orders but always has to try to gain the family's agreement to the order.[14] If the judge overrides the family's views without good reason, this constitutes grounds for appeal. If an order is made, parents retain their parental authority, but the judge can regulate their contact, or provisionally suspend contact, if the interests of the child require.[15] Only in a higher court can a judge terminate contact. It is also virtually impossible, and for the French research participants unheard of, for a child to be adopted against the wishes of the parents. The powers of the Judge for Children are wide and flexible, but ultimately more limited than the powers of the magistrates and judges in the English system. The parents have the right to be legally represented but very rarely are because the system promotes and facilitates communication and dialogue between them and the judge. The audience with the judge is an informal discussion using lay language, and includes the social worker as another interested party rather than as a main protagonist.

The legal framework therefore reflects the fact that the community knows what is expected of parents, knows that the judge can take action to enforce

103

standards; but also knows that the judge must try to work with the parents' agreement, and cannot finally sever all connection between parent and child. Enormous emphasis is placed on the need to keep children in their families or, if they are removed, to return them. The family has a reality in France that is much stronger than in England; the child is part of the family, and there is nothing that one can do to change that fact. So, one has to try to change the family. The French legal system reflects that reality.

*Adoption and long-term placement*
The French social workers were extremely surprised by the concept of adoption as a long-term solution for children. The French attitude to the family makes it hard for them to envisage a child never returning home. When a long-term solution is necessary, they see fostering or residential care as the answer. The French were interested in the development of open adoption, but though their *adoption simple* would lend itself to this, they still found it difficult to accept. They gave more weight to the suffering that a child experiences on being separated from carers, whether birth or foster family, and this influenced their planning.

The English social workers felt that a child had a right to be brought up in a family, and that another family could be a viable substitute for the family of origin. This difference of opinion was strongly held, and was very little modified on either side by exposure to each others' views. It crystallised the differing cultural expectations of the family in the two countries, and it demonstrated how powerfully these expectations affected the structures within which the workers operated. Just as the legal system of child protection reflects a particular concept of the family, so also does the way and the direction in which services develop. The most highly developed and labour intensive services in France were, first, the services for work in the community (both within the family and in the wider community through the *équipe de prévention*)[16] and, second, the residential child care services. Fostering, although extensive, was less well developed and adoption was not in the picture.

*Supervision and management structures*
Michelle's team was in a small, specialist organisation and there are problems in making direct comparisons with a social services children and

families team. However, it is worth noting that the combination of team support, management by the team leader and professional supervision by the psychologist were felt by her and her colleagues to be effective. A more direct comparison can be made with the support and supervision available to the social workers in the DASS, where they are part of a multidisciplinary team including health visitors, doctors in community health, specialist and generic social workers and psychologists. Teams are area based and meet about once a fortnight. Any member of the team can bring a case for discussion, and decisions are team based, which is considered very important. This enables early sharing of information with a range of different workers involved. If it is felt that a specialist ASE team should be involved, this is decided by the team and discussed at a meeting of the team with the ASE Inspector.

Our research suggests that many of the decisions made in the UK by the team leader are made in France by the multidisciplinary team and the more complex decisions that in the UK might involve the area manager are likely to be made by the team meeting with the ASE Inspector.[17] The Inspector has the final decision-making power, but the decision is taken in the context of the team. There is very little management supervision, and professional supervision is either team based or provided by the psychologist. On hearing what was expected of an English team leader, one of the French workers commented on the role as being 'at once manager, supervisor and social worker intervening with the family', and asked how one person could be expected to have the expertise to fill all these roles.

To summarise, the French social services have a flat team-based management hierarchy while the English have a steep individually based hierarchy. One English participant, commenting on the work of his French colleague, said that 'the need to liaise with other professions slows things down, but shares accountability, which makes for less anxiety ... the slowness doesn't seem to lead to disaster, so maybe that doesn't matter'.

These key differences illustrate the complexities of the differences in the structure and culture of the two systems. It is possible for one aspect of difference to relate to both structure and culture. For example, the French Civil Code, for which we have no equivalent, both sets up a different legal structure and expresses a difference of culture. Adoption provides another example. The structure offers wider possibilities than the culture accepts.

French adoption law could be used for open adoption (*adoption simple*), but this would not be culturally acceptable. The different elements are closely entwined and there is a perpetual interplay between structure, culture and functioning.

The judicial system expresses the relationship between the family and the community, and at the same time affects the way in which workers carry out their tasks. The social workers, who are part of the community, share the same expectations of the family and work within those expectations. This affects their allocation of time and resources. The way in which the system functions feeds back and reinforces the structure. Michelle and the ASE Inspector both acted on the unspoken assumption that it was better to risk possible sexual abuse rather than remove Genevieve from her family. Viv thought that in England the risk of abuse would have weighed more heavily against the disruption of the family and that legal action (a Section 47 investigation) would have been necessary. This would have made it extremely difficult to engage the family. Michelle and Viv did not differ in their assessment of the risks, but they did differ in their valuation of the family.

**Implications for practice**

Developing ideas for our own practice from other countries is not a simple matter. Transplanting part of a foreign structure is likely to produce unforeseen results when located in a system with different cultural assumptions. The case example used above was chosen because it does not demonstrate an easy road to success. It shows that risk taking is difficult, time-consuming and may not lead to a clear evaluation of the risks. After a year and a bit, Michelle could feel that M Laville had shown some trust in her, and had taken the important step of talking about his inappropriate behaviour; but in many respects the situation had not changed much and Genevieve was not able to talk about what had happened. There were plans for a constructive placement for Genevieve, but Bernard and Cecile were still at home, M Laville was still drinking, and Mme Laville was still depressed. If the English system is to move towards a more preventive and therapeutic way of working with families, then these are necessary risks which have to be placed in a context of long-term support. Michelle was continuing to work with the family and there were no signs that the case would be closed. The family was receiving a great deal of support and through this was being monitored.

Preventive social work is long term and frequently, by its very nature, inconclusive. Its successes are likely to be invisible; even its failures are not clear cut as worse might have happened. Our culture is intolerant of things that are open ended, hard to measure and hard to quantify. Reintroducing preventive social work to a system which has for some years been dominated by legal discourse[18] and a political culture of non-intervention[19] is not simple without changing structures. However, this is not impossible. If we go back to the list of key differences that affected the way Michelle worked, what suggestions for change might we develop?

*Resources*
Resources for preventive work are fewer than in France. This may be because a high proportion is allocated to court work and child protection, but there may also be a lower level overall. If preventive work is to be achieved, whether by reallocation or increase, more resources are needed.

*Entering the judicial system*
Barriers to involving the authority of the law in England are many and diverse. Among them are cost, the effect of Section 1(5) of the Children Act 1989, and the conflictive and adversarial nature of the process. One result of this is that social workers have little opportunity to use supervision orders to support work with families before a child is removed from home. The informal and nonadversarial functioning of the French Family Court demonstrates that even with the reforms of the Children Act 1989, the court process in this country remains intimidating and judgmental, alien and often traumatic to the families who encounter it.

*The duty to investigate*
The English system is unusual among European systems in that it involves the social worker heavily in the investigation of child abuse. It is also unusual in putting such a heavy emphasis on investigation as a prime consideration.[20] It is not only French social workers who see this as problematic. The emphasis on investigation affects the distribution of resources and the potential for working in partnership with parents. It

would be hard in the climate of public opinion seemingly always ready to blame social workers, for local authorities to step back from the imperative of the duty to investigate. But it is also hard to see how, unless they do, they can release the resources and energy to work preventively. In addition, it is hard to see how social workers can build trust and a basis for working in partnership with families if they so frequently start their work on an investigative basis.

## Management structure

The management of social workers is strikingly different in France. In general, French workers in the project were less anxious about their role and more confident in taking risks. A consensual, nonhierarchical way of working within the organisations seemed to reflect a way of working with families based on dialogue, discussion and negotiation. Adopting a less hierarchical management style and separating management supervision from professional supervision could facilitate a more flexible and less adversarial way of working with families.

## The importance of process

These reflections have a unifying principle: they are connected by a focus on the process of work, on the manner in which things take place, on the "how" rather than the "what". In this way of working, procedures take second place to flexibility and negotiation. Whatever the specific changes that we might make, the chances of success are slight unless we can achieve a change of perspective that gives primary importance to process rather than procedures.

The Children Act 1989 is predicated on the importance of the family and of maintaining the family. It therefore came as something of a surprise to find that the concept of the family informing our work is different from, and less substantial than, the concept of the family in France. The strength of the commitment of English social workers to the idea that children need *a* family seems, when seen from across the Channel, to have as its corollary a lesser commitment to the importance for the child of their own family.[21]

Working preventively and therapeutically with children within their families entails a level of acceptance of the family as it is, and a readiness to believe in the possibility of change. In order to build a working relationship within which families trust social workers, maybe social workers must feel able to trust families. At the same time we must recognise that all cultures draw different lines round the family, and that any changes we might want to make will be affected not only by the legal and administrative structures within which we make them, but also by the assumptions and expectations of our culture.

## References

1   Cooper A, Hetherington R, Baistow K, Pitts J, and Spriggs A, *Positive Child Protection: A view from abroad*, Russell House Publishing, 1995.

2   See 1 above.

3   Hetherington R, Cooper A, and Grevot G, *The French Child Protection System*, Centre for Comparative Social Work Studies, West London Institute, 1993.

4   See 1 above.

5   Ely P, and Stanley C, *The French Alternative: Delinquency, prevention and child protection in France*, NACRO, 1990.

6   See 5 above.

7   White R, Carr P, and Lowe N, *A Guide to the Children Act 1989*, Butterworths, 1990.

8   Parton N, *Governing the Family: Child care, child protection and the state*, Macmillan, 1991.

9   See 8 above.

10  See 8 above.

11  Audit Commission, *Seen but not Heard: Co-ordinating community child health and social services for children in need*, HMSO, 1994.

12  Civil Code Art. 371–2.

13  See 5 above.

14    Civil Code Art. 375–1.

15    Civil Code Art. 375–7.

16    Hetherington R, "Trans-manche Partnerships", *Adoption & Fostering*, 18:3, BAAF, 1994.

17    Research in progress.

18    King M, and Piper C, *How the Law thinks about Children*, Gower, 1990.

19    See 8 above.

20    Research in progress.

21    See 1 above.

# 10 The confidential doctor system
## An appraisal

*Sarah Borthwick and Barbara Hutchinson*

*Sarah Borthwick is a Trainer/Consultant in and Manager of BAAF's Southern Region. Barbara Hutchinson is a Trainer/Consultant in BAAF's Northern Region.*

This chapter aims to describe the Confidential Doctor system in Belgium, of which the child protection arm, the *Kind in Nood* (Child in Need) is a part. It is based on a three-day visit to the Brussels Centre by the authors. They compare the systems in the two countries and explain the relevance of the Confidential Doctor approach to the United Kingdom.

### The development of *Kind in Nood* in Brussels

The Confidential Doctor Centre *Kind in Nood* offers an alternative and therapeutic approach to dealing with child protection. The centre aims to respond to children and families where abuse has or may have occurred without recourse to any civil or criminal proceedings. Unlike the child protection system in the UK, the centre does not refer child abuse cases to, or work jointly with, the police leading to criminal investigations or prosecutions. It will, however, support individuals in families if they wish to go to the police. On occasion, it may also obtain orders from the civil court to ensure a child's protection – six per cent of all cases it deals with – and even in these circumstances, it will not breach confidentiality.

The centres developed across Belgium in the early 1980s as a response to perceived failures and difficulties within the child protection system at that time. That system bore many similarities to practice and procedures in the UK. For example, considerable emphasis was placed on investigating and identifying offenders, at the end of which few criminal prosecutions resulted. Moreover, many families were "coerced" into therapy by the threat of removal of their children or prosecution if they failed to comply.

A number of professionals in Belgium challenged this system. They argued that the role of child protection workers as both social controllers and therapists led to conflict and authoritarianism, often mirroring abusive relationships within families.[1] They questioned the criminal process in relation to prosecuting offenders who, because of evidential difficulties, were rarely taken to court. They recognised that, in cases that did reach the courtroom, many child witnesses and their families were further traumatised by the legal process itself.

A group of key consultants therefore implemented an alternative theoretical model. In this model, which is currently used, the risk of prosecution of parents or carers is largely removed, and a therapeutic response to children and families free of punishment or coercion is offered. This approach encourages parents and children to come for help of their own free will, without fear of judgement; the need for denial of abuse is thereby reduced.

The first centres were set up in several Belgian cities and towns and were based on the Dutch model. The centres are located in hospital settings and are directed by a consultant psychiatrist leading a multi-disciplinary team of professionals. These teams generally include social workers, psychologists, nurses, speech therapists and health visitors, although there are individual differences across centres. Services offered include crisis intervention and telephone counselling, child, individual couple and family therapy, and residential accommodation in the hospital. Foster care is arranged by the centres, using local agencies. The centres also offer support and counselling to professionals involved in child protection work, together with training, information and research.

The Confidential Doctor Centre in Brussels University Hospital receives a considerable number of referrals and deals with all aspects of child abuse and neglect, including child sexual abuse. Whatever the problem, parents or carers admitting to abuse or neglect are not referred to the police and are guaranteed absolute confidentiality.

The aim is to help the parents understand themselves as children and adults, acknowledge their action, and take responsibility for not harming their children in the future. In an analysis of the cases seen by the Brussels Centre in 1992, Marneffe[2] reports that out of 110 cases, 102 perpetrators acknowledged the abuse. Therapeutic work was carried out with these individuals. Additionally, emphasis was placed on supporting the non-abusing parent's capacity to protect the children in the future.

In the main, families remain living together or children are reunited during or after therapeutic work. There have been a few severe cases of abuse where no agreement for working together could be reached and, as previously mentioned, civil proceedings were initiated in order to secure protection of the children. There is follow-up of families over a considerable length of time, and children and families are encouraged to come back should difficulties develop again.

The Brussels Centre is now funded by the Social Welfare Department, giving it political and financial backing. Prior to 1989, there was no government support and funding was inadequate. Acceptance and recognition has come through its achievements and the commitment shown by dedicated professionals.

With its emphasis on genuine partnership, the Confidential Doctor system presents a real challenge to those established child protection systems which are both controlling and caring within rigidly defined legal procedures.

The major questions are: Does the Confidential Doctor system work? Does it reduce the risk of reabuse for children? Is it possible to work with sex offenders in such a trusting way? Isn't violence towards children a crime? Does the system have relevance for the UK? These are questions we hoped to find answers to during our visit to the Brussels Centre.

**The visit**

We had both heard Catherine Marneffe, the then Director of the Centre, speak at the BAAF Medical Group Seminar on Child Protection in Europe in 1992 and had found her refreshing and challenging. The Confidential Doctor system she advocated and directed at the time appeared to be so radically different from the child protection practice and procedures in the UK that, when the opportunity arose to visit the Brussels Centre, we did not hesitate.

As BAAF trainers, we run a variety of training courses in child protection work in the south and north of England. As practitioners ourselves, we share the dissatisfaction of many of our colleagues in relevant disciplines with the current system of child protection. Our main criticisms include the focus on investigation, the seeming ineffectiveness of the criminal process and the lack of therapeutic work for children and families. Rules surrounding an investigative interview with a child seem to block rather than facilitate the possibility of disclosure. The resources provided for the investigative aspect of child protection seem heavily to outweigh any work in prevention and education, in helping families to care appropriately for their children, and in supporting foster and adoptive placements where necessary.

University Hospital in Brussels is in the outskirts of the city and is easily accessible by bus. *Kind in Nood* is located in the Children's Hospital which is modern, well-resourced, and non-stigmatising. All the members of the child protection team have their own offices which are suitably equipped to be child-centred.

We spent considerable time over the three days with team members including the then Director, who is also a consultant psychiatrist, and Annik Lampo, another consultant psychiatrist. We also spoke to psychologists, a social worker, and a speech therapist who were all part of the apparently strong and committed multidisciplinary team. We were impressed with the high level of professional practice as we discussed roles, practice issues, and the underlying systemic philosophy behind the centre's work.

Most families are seen at the centre for therapy. There are a high number of self-referrals as well as referrals from agencies. All members of the family are seen, both individually and together. If children do not wish to meet with their parents, they do not do so until they feel able to. More than one therapist is involved with the same family: one worker for the child and a worker for each parent. Each professional in the team has developed skills in specific areas of work such as working with children, nonabusing and abusing parents; crisis intervention; long-term therapy; and speech therapy. However, roles are not rigidly defined according to profession. For example, the speech therapist has a wide role. As speech therapy is generally perceived by parents as non-threatening and useful for their children, it is often accepted. Then, while the children's speech and language improves, the therapist can be a valuable medium for helping parents to understand and respond to their child's emotional needs. In some cases, this has worked better than the conventional therapy aimed at achieving such understanding.

114

## Our impressions

We found our visit inspiring, offering as it did a refreshing change from the legal and procedure-weighted system we had left behind. On reflection, we still had some outstanding questions and uncertainties about both systems but thought that the Belgian system offered a valuable corrective to the current system in the UK. The first major impact on us was the sense of optimism which underpins the work of the team. The children referred have usually experienced serious physical, sexual or emotional abuse as more minor incidents are usually dealt with elsewhere. The team believes that in 80 per cent of the cases, the child can be returned to the family home with patterns of family functioning modified sufficiently to keep the child safe. Families often remain together. Where one or more people leave the family home, this decision is taken by the family. It is not a condition imposed by professionals or a court. The team continues its involvement with families over a long period, which enabled staff to tell us with confidence that the incidence of reabuse is low.

Our second realisation was that abusers are not seen as people apart. There is no sense that two distinct categories have been created, i.e., abusers and non-abusers. Rather there is an acknowledgement that the capacity for abuse lies within us all. Therefore, individuals are seen as being along a continuum of "more to less likely" to abuse. The workers believe that individuals can move in either direction along this continuum in response to a variety of factors. This is in marked contrast to the view, prevalent in the UK, that sexually abusive behaviour in particular is addictive, compulsive and resistant to modification. The *Kind in Nood* team accepts that this is true of some sexual abusers but sees them as being at the extreme end of the continuum. The attention paid to physical and emotional abuse and neglect was a timely reminder. The team is acutely aware that physical abuse and neglect can end in death; they also indicate that children who experience physical abuse are damaged emotionally in much the same way as those who are sexually abused. Is it possible that we in the UK are now so alert to sexual abuse that we fail to respond appropriately to children who have been (only) physically assaulted or neglected?

"Partnership", a term much in vogue in UK social work circles, truly underlies the work of *Kind in Nood*. The team starts from the assumption

115

that most parents care about their children and their approach shows concern rather than accusation or inquisition. A starting point with a parent who has injured a child might be, 'You obviously have difficulties in the way you respond to your child. How do you think we might help you change this?'

The team aims to build up the parents' motivation to change. They ask parents for suggestions as to how to change the situation in such a way as to keep the child safe. They encourage parents to take the responsibility for apologising to the child, explaining what happened and what will change in the future.

The guarantee of confidentiality given to parents lessens the need for denial. In consequence, there is a high rate of admission and sustained denial is rare. However, time is an essential ingredient in helping parents through the process of admitting and confronting what they have done to their children.

A typical approach to a parent would be, 'I am concerned about what has happened to your child. I wonder why you are not concerned? You must be worried, especially as you cannot explain what happened. How are you going to keep your child safe in the future if you don't know how he or she got hurt this time? Let's talk about what might have happened.' This sort of conversation might continue over a sustained period, reinforced by assurances that the parent's genuine concern is recognised.

The strategy of returning abused children to their families carries a high degree of risk. Although we were told that the results of long-term follow-up are reassuring, we were also told that one child had died. To contain the anxiety produced by such risk-taking work, individual workers need the support of the whole team. This particular multi-disciplinary team is stable and well-established. Our impression was that its members have a real regard for each other and respect each other's area of expertise. Individually and collectively, the team is confident in its own abilities. The striking contrast between the situation of this team and any counterpart in the UK is that the work is not undermined by public hostility – social work being valued rather than derided by the public. The absence of a sensationalist tabloid press is also significant. There have been no high-profile abuse enquiries such as have followed the deaths of children in the UK.

It was also striking that the team seemed unaware of the possibility of an allegation of abuse being made against one of them, and both male and female therapists worked individually with individual abused children behind closed doors. It is interesting that not a single allegation of abuse has been made. Contrast this with the real and well-founded anxiety experienced by workers and carers in the UK.

**Questions and reservations**
Without doubt we were impressed by the work of *Kind in Nood* of the Confidential Doctor Centre. However, we did have some questions and some reservations.

- The team claimed to use diverse methods of working with abusers and abused children, yet they appeared to be firmly grounded in the dysfunctional family/individual pathology model.
- The strong emphasis on enabling mothers to take responsibility for protecting their child carries an inherent danger of allowing those who would blame mothers to find support for their views in cases of failure.
- We wonder if their approach to child sexual abuse risks "minimalisation" of sexual abuse in some instances, and whether therapists are sometimes "seduced" into unconscious collusion by some of the abusers.
- Both individually and collectively, the team seemed to be unaware of cultural issues in their analysis of abusive families and their approach to abused children. We were told that the minority ethnic population of Belgium, although small, is represented in disproportionately small numbers in the centre's patients. None the less, when we looked for play materials and literature addressing the needs of children from minority ethnic communities, we found none.

At the time of our visit, the team was dealing with the aftermath of the child's death. We received the impression that this tragedy could lead to a review of their work, always important when new ideas are put into practice.

**Relevance for the UK**
Does the Confidential Doctor Centre's approach have any relevance for practitioners in the UK? It is hard to imagine two more diverse systems. The UK now has a highly sophisticated child protection network. Responses to

117

official inquiries following a number of deaths of abused children have produced an ever tighter and more regimented system. This system *does* offer some protection to some children and has increased social workers' – as well as public – understanding of some aspects of abusive behaviour. Yet the cry – this must never be allowed to happen again – is usually followed after some time by another death or scandal, another inquiry, and yet another set of recommendations.

Paradoxically, the very system which offers some protection to children may also prove equally or even more abusive to them. Once a child discloses abuse to a professional, it appears that a juggernaut is set in motion, which then cannot be stopped. Frequently families are split up and the children find themselves either being removed from the only secure base they know, or being blamed for precipitating the removal of another family member. We exhort each other to listen to the child but we ignore the child who says she or he did not wish us to act in this way, but only wanted the abuse to stop. Distress and damage are compounded by introducing children into the care system in which they may experience repeated moves and which leaves them vulnerable to reabuse.

The UK system is constrained by the needs of the court, whether it be the Family Proceedings Court or the criminal court. This judicial approach entrenches denial, minimises the chance of movement or change by the perpetrator, and produces few criminal prosecutions. Furthermore, emphasis on detection rather than prevention or treatment swallows up huge resources of workers and finance, resources which are then not available for other work with children and families. In short, the UK system appears to be about blame rather than change, and at times workers are understandably as much concerned with self-protection as with child protection.

Are the best aspects of the Confidential Doctor system transferable to the UK? Would we wish to change our approach? Certainly we would not wish to lose the gains we have made. Yet there is no apparent reason why abusers in the UK should be less open to change than those in Belgium, or why it should not be equally possible to return children home quickly and safely. The Confidential Doctor system is dependent on well trained, well supported and well equipped practitioners and perhaps it is not possible to replicate this with less thoroughly trained, supported and equipped staff. Nevertheless, similar approaches in other European countries using different groups of workers appear to be having positive results.

To move from a judicial to a welfare model in the UK would entail a significant change of mindset on the part of both policy makers and practitioners. But a growing dissatisfaction with the present system is discernible. Is there a British Confidential Doctor system already in embryo?

## References

1 Marneffe C, 'The Confidential Doctor Centre – a new approach to child protection work', *Adoption & Fostering*, 16:4, BAAF, 1992.

2 See 1 above.

# 11   Taking a grip on the debate

## Ruth Gardner

*Ruth Gardner is Services Development Manager (under 12s) with the London Borough of Hackney, responsible for the development of Family Support and for Child Protection. She has worked in both voluntary and statutory sectors, as a manager and in research and development.*

The range of views, questions and hypotheses set out in the preceding papers represent a significant debate. It is a search by professionals from different disciplines for improvement to our current approach to child protection. No simple solutions are offered. The true state of current practice is reflected here. The "givens", that is, structured interventions to identify harm and to protect children, are under close scrutiny. In time, perhaps, they will be dismantled and reassembled, but at present different perspectives abound. The one constant is a degree of anxiety and un-certainty, particularly for those who must attempt to operate the system.

It would be unhelpful for me to try and impose a false consensus onto this debate. Rather, I want first to identify some themes which present as dilemmas and second, to ask whether those concerned with child protec-tion, for instance, members of Area Child Protection Committees (ACPCs), could take a grip on the debate by together exploring these themes more actively, thus restoring confidence in their practice. Delegates to the lively workshop which initiated this book preferred this route rather than hoping that the controversy would simply die down.

### The implications of the Children Act 1989
Several contributors to the book demonstrate the now widespread unease with our highly proceduralised and litigious child protection procedures. The Children Act perfectly demonstrates a central dilemma in social welfare – policing versus service – its horns tipped towards the former. The duty to investigate harm is extended and reinforced, backed by detailed guidance which 'should be complied with unless (there are) exceptional reasons'.

The service element of the Act, Part III, despite exhortations from the Department of Health, is riddled with loopholes and qualifications and much of it remains discretionary. At a time when local government financing has been under unprecedented pressure, the Act was said to have 'no resource implications'. It has never been fully accepted that there must be such implications in 'working together', implying as it does more sensitive investigations and inquiries which involve responding to needs.

## Taking risks

As Tunstill and Atherton point out in Chapter 4, the Government, local councillors and senior managers should support one another in acknowledging that no system, including the care system, can ever be risk-free. A less intrusive approach in working with families, as Robinson states in Chapter 3, may mean that some concerns are not investigated rigorously, but a heavier approach can deter families from seeking help until too late – the help they desperately need. It might even result in children entering care against their long-term interests. There is no doubt that many people, however misguidedly, see social services primarily as rescuing children by removal, rather than as offering support to families.

## Thresholds for defining need and harm

The thresholds we currently use to define need and harm must be openly articulated and debated, not left to the establishment by individual practitioners. Clearly there is little consensus even in the House of Lords, where, as Spicer's chapter indicates, two out of the five Law Lords feared that the approach followed by the majority would make it difficult to protect children at risk of abuse. These complex issues need clarification both for practitioners and for the public. It is useless to draw attention to these matters after a child has died. With hindsight, matters are highlighted which almost invariably appear to point towards such a stark and unacceptable event. In reality most situations are open to the application of just such varying thresholds as mentioned above, outcomes rarely being at all predictable.

## The emphasis on investigation: the role of social services

It is probably true that the net effect of tight procedures, fraught debates on children's versus parents' rights and official inquiries have thrown doubt upon social services' discretion as lead agencies. As a result, greater dependence has been laid on police investigative skills and on legal advice. The results are mixed. There may well be less short-term risk to the child, and certainly to the reputation of the agency. There may also be better interdisciplinary work in preparing a case for court. On the other hand, investigation is not necessarily safer for the child in the long-term and it offers families no guarantee of welfare or support. Legal processes such as the use of authority, precedent and the evaluation of fact, are important; but equally important are mutual respect and partnership, joint planning in day-to-day work, advocacy for needs to be met and balancing the interests, wishes and feelings of all involved. Although these processes are legally sanctioned they tend to be subordinated to investigation. Creativity is needed to deal with the individuality of each situation and risk – albeit calculated risk is always involved. Social services and partner agencies need to affirm this and to reject both the extreme labels of being 'weak and woolly' or 'social police'.

**The emphasis on investigation: the role of the police**
Concerns about the procedural approach voiced here include the effects of greater police involvement. Despite the usually sensitive approach of the police in this area of work, parents will inevitably be stigmatised while only a tiny proportion will, or should, be prosecuted. Searches for evidence and the construction of cases for court devour resources, often at the expense of any immediate or planned response to the child's and family's needs. It is in these early days of waiting that secondary abuse or system abuse can begin, not necessarily in terms of direct harm but because the focus is on the adult drama and not on the child's needs. The paramountcy principle is undermined in these circumstances, to the detriment of work with the child and the family.

This is not an argument against essential interventions, which can sometimes galvanise support; it is rather an argument against the intervention as an end in itself. These concerns are supported by research indicating that in case conferences most time is spent on the harm incident and the decision whether or not to register, while much less is spent on inter-agency protection plans and consideration of how family needs will be assessed and met.[1] In Chapter 7 Gerrilyn Smith suggests that the tight controls around disclosure and investigation, dictated by rules of evidence, may offer professionals a sense of security, but at the same time it militates against some children speaking out as they wish and need to. We certainly do not at present have the means to help either adult or young abusers to change their behaviour, yet this would be one of the most positive preventive moves. A first step in this direction must be to shift public awareness beyond the need to apportion blame.

## Degrees of protection

Nearly all contributors to the book see a broader-based contextualised approach to child protection as an urgent priority and various elements of this approach are discussed. For a start, the very terms "protection" and "harm" recall their precursors, "rescue" and "abuse", specifically refer-ring to the removal of a child from a parent or parents who inflict serious harm. In terms of immediate protection it appears that the system is relatively successful with children at this extreme end of the spectrum, but in wider child welfare terms it is less so, as many remain behaviourally disturbed whatever their placement. Lower socioeconomic status is sig-nificantly associated with poorer outcomes whether or not there has been a history of harm, yet ironically, women who have separated to escape abuse also face these risks.[2] Therefore it is time for those operating current sys-tems to carefully examine definitions and aims. The aims of many ACPCs are more concerned with maintaining joint procedures than with raising public awareness, research into outcomes, establishing standards for joint work, or addressing areas of need and risk, for example, domestic violence.

## Partnership with parents

We also need to examine the preferred settings for advice and support. It may be that schools, health centres or places in the community are more appropriate venues in some situations than social services offices or home visits.

Again, the current process of referral, home visit, strategy discussion, and so on should focus much more on *how* needs will be identified and resources assessed. This should include the family and the 'community of adults who protect' and should have the twin aims of increasing both the safety and the welfare of the family as a unit. The use of Family Group Conferences and Needs Assessment meetings with families is positive, but attention must be given to the whole process involving families from the manner of referral to outcome and evaluation. Currently, each stage of practice seems to be an isolated, closed event rather than part of an open, learning and research process. According to Gibbons et al, 'more intensive and prolonged social work contact as well as packages including treatment for an adult, therapeutic attendance at a family centre and support from a voluntary agency, all appear to have benefits for children remaining with their parents'.[3] This gives impetus to creating support services along the lines suggested by Tunstill and Atherton in Chapter 4. Robinson says in Chapter 3 that 'family support is not prevention of abuse'; we should test this out and also note that child protection, as it is currently understood, is not necessarily prevention either. Between a quarter and a third of children in the national studies had been re-abused.[4] We know that many family support programmes do indeed reduce parental stress and improve parent-child relations; that even small degrees of day care can be highly effective.[5] We also know informally that such initiatives are associated with local reductions in child protection registration. But we face real difficulty in that a successful preventive development is not usually reinforced with new resources. In the current public sector climate, it can be used to justify a reduction in some other part of the service. It cannot be a choice between prevention and support or good, responsive crisis services or treatment and therapy; the whole continuum has to be present. That crises which are successfully prevented one month may present again a few months later is not a failure, but a fact of life in human services.

**Different models of procedure and response**
In this context, the accounts given by Hetherington of the French model in Chapter 9 and by Borthwick and Hutchinson of the Belgian "Confidential Doctor" system in Chapter 10, deserve close attention. Different cultures and systems, including the experience of our own minority communities, generally receive short shrift here. The Confidential Doctor model, while traditional in a therapeutic sense, seems to provide voluntary and non-stigmatising access to help for family members. Where a child or young person has been abused, it can help him or her individually and the family

124

collectively to find a way forward. Presumably some families may use therapy privately in the UK for these purposes without social services involvement, but this is not a formalised response to child protection concerns. There is a presumption in both models described that families stay together in all but the worst scenarios. Hence the possibility exists that the child may not be heard and that one parent, in some instances, is given unrealistic responsibility for protecting children. However, in England, where there is a greater likelihood of the response being removal of the child, or the abuser and/or prosecution, these problems have not been eliminated. Mothers continue to feel unsupported and children who want the abuse to stop – but also want contact between family members – are often not heard. The importance of speech therapy in the Belgian multi-disciplinary approach is interesting, in that it helps give children confidence in communicating both in general and specifically about what has happened. This contrasts with Lynch's concern in Chapter 5 that the paediatrician's contribution to child protection here has become narrowly forensic, possibly putting doctors off paediatrics altogether but certainly resulting in a missed opportunity for a crucial assessment of health needs to prevent longer-term harm.

The possibility for closely co-ordinated and joint service provision across agencies is potentially the most exciting development of recent years. It must not lead to the loss of already scarce resources or boundary squabbles but rather to creative joint targets for populations of children in need and the pooling of skills and cash to meet the need.

### In summary

We have a number of issues currently heightened to the point where practitioners could feel paralysed by difficult decisions. As a result, yet more official guidance will be sought. These dilemmas are concerned with:

- balancing the rights and interests of the child and family members whenever a decision is taken;
- the immediate and longer-term welfare of the child;
- the possibility of unpredictable change which with hindsight can make even well-justified decisions appear poor;
- finding the right level and threshold so that action is neither neglectful and dismissive of real concerns, nor intrusive and damaging;

- lack of investment in service development, evaluation and skills transfer.

People dealing with this work need:
- better public awareness and a clearer mandate from the community;
- high quality information and access to expert training, supervision and advice;
- knowledge that family members can each receive good independent advocacy;
- a range of tested family support and treatment services, both universal and specialised.
- central and local politicians to acknowledge the value, and the real costs, of improving services for children in need.

Contributions in this book indicate that we are still actively struggling with these issues and trying to find new ways forward across professional and agency boundaries, difficult though this will always be. This is the legacy of painful enquiries and hard work of the past few decades, but it will ensure that, in time, we *do* achieve better results for children and families.

### References

1   Farmer E, and Owen M, *Child Protection Practice: Private risks and public remedies*, HMSO, 1995.

2   Gibbons J, Gallagher B, Bell C, and Gordon D, *Development after Physical Abuse in Early Childhood: A follow-up study of children on protection registers*, HMSO, 1995

3   See 2 above.

4   *Child Protection and Abuse: Messages from research*, HMSO, 1995.

5   Gibbons J, Thorpe S, and Wilkinson P, *Family Support and Prevention: Studies in local areas*, HMSO, 1990.